MW00488440

"Three things strike me about Barry Gibson's work. First, it is refreshingly Christ-centered, full of biblical wisdom and examples throughout church history. Second, Gibson shows that repentance, though vital in beginning the Christian life, characterizes the whole. Finally, Gibson shows how Christians turn from sin and follow Christ through being firmly planted in his church. May all who read this book daily 'repent . . . that times of refreshing may come from the presence of the Lord' (Acts 3:19 ESV)."

—**OREN R. MARTIN**, senior director of
equipping, Watermark Community Church

"Thanks to Barry Gibson's *The Power of Repentance*, we have a clear definition, explanation, illustration, and application of the doctrine of repentance in an easy-to-understand format. I especially appreciate his emphasis on not only the personal side of repentance, but how it relates to the Christian community. This book is not just for individual reading, but would also be a blessing to any church where it is studied in a small group setting."

—**DONALD S, WHITNEY**, professor of biblical spirituality and
associate dean, The Southern Baptist Theological Seminary

"'Inconceivable' is the oft repeated mantra of Vizzini (*The Princess Bride*). His misuse of that adjective is challenged by Inigo Montoya who retorts, 'I don't think that means what you think it means.' Likewise, 'Repent' is often a misdefined and misapplied command by well-meaning preachers. Barry Gibson meticulously defines, convincingly illustrates, scripturally supports, and practically applies what it means to repent. Read this book!"

—**ED MOORE**, pastor, North Shore Baptist Church

"In *The Power of Repentance,* Barry Gibson employs a full arsenal of biblical exegesis, church history, and powerful illustrations and quotes from some of Christendom's most important thinkers to communicate a robust understanding of biblical repentance rooted in the gospel of grace. Gibson's writing style is such that this work will well serve both the new believer and the veteran pastor. From here on, I will not preach on repentance without consulting this important work."

—**BRIAN PAYNE**, senior pastor, Lakeview Baptist Church

"What makes this book so powerful is its ability to pinpoint the essential truths of biblical repentance with convicting clarity and Christlike gentleness. Grounded solidly in the Scriptures and drawing upon the wisest theologians, Barry Gibson helps us see into the inner-workings of the heart-altering turnaround that divinely delivers us from a 'life that displeased God toward a life that joyfully engages toward a direction that pleases him!'"

—**LAURIE AKER**, executive director, Thistlebend Ministries

The Power of Repentance

The Power of Repentance

How God Changes Lives

Barry J. Gibson

Foreword by Thomas R. Schreiner

WIPF & STOCK · Eugene, Oregon

THE POWER OF REPENTANCE
How God Changes Lives

Copyright © 2023 Barry J. Gibson. All rights reserved. Except for brief quotations in critical publications or reviews, no part of this book may be reproduced in any manner without prior written permission from the publisher. Write: Permissions, Wipf and Stock Publishers, 199 W. 8th Ave., Suite 3, Eugene, OR 97401.

Wipf & Stock
An Imprint of Wipf and Stock Publishers
199 W. 8th Ave., Suite 3
Eugene, OR 97401

www.wipfandstock.com

PAPERBACK ISBN: 978-1-6667-5343-1
HARDCOVER ISBN: 978-1-6667-5344-8
EBOOK ISBN: 978-1-6667-5345-5

VERSION NUMBER 10/06/23

Dedicated to my wife, Julie, whose life displays
authentic repentance, and her undying support
was integral in bringing this work to fruition.

Contents

Foreword

Thomas R. Schreiner

Too often in evangelical circles the importance of repentance is neglected, as if it is an unimportant sideline in the New Testament. But Jesus began his preaching ministry with an announcement that the kingdom had come, and in response people should believe in the good news and repent (Mark 1:15). Barry Gibson, in this wonderfully clear book, reminds us how important repentance is, and he defines repentance for us so that we avoid a superficial understanding. Repentance isn't merely changing bad habits in our lives. When we repent, we turn the entirety of our lives over to Jesus Christ and acknowledge in reality that he is Lord. Nor should we think of repentance only in terms of turning our lives around, though it involves that. Biblical repentance means that we turn to the Lord, that we give ourselves to him. In other words, repentance is deeply personal in that we turn from our sins and give ourselves wholly to Jesus Christ.

Gibson also rightly emphasizes that true repentance shows up in our lives in the way that we live. Repentance is not an abstraction from how we live day by day and moment by moment. Martin Luther declared that the Christian life is one of daily repentance. We can easily begin to think that we repented once at our conversion and now we can leave repentance behind. But if we are living in God's sight and humbly before him, then we continue to see our sin, and by God's grace we feel sorrow for it and turn from it. Sometimes people describe the Christian life in terms of spiritual breathing, and part of that breathing, as we are sensitive to the Holy Spirit, is repentance. Of course, our repentance doesn't save us; only God saves us, but our repentance reveals whether we truly belong to God.

Another feature of Gibson's book that is striking is the importance of the local church in our life of repentance. So often in our independent spirit we think that we can live the Christian life alone apart from any others. The New Testament teaches us that we need each other, that we won't live according to God's will unless we are vitally involved with other believers. As we interact with others, we see in fresh ways what it means for us to repent and to give ourselves entirely to God. Gibson also provides sage advice in our interactions with unbelievers, giving us a sample prayer that we can voice before God for the sake of those who don't embrace Jesus as Lord and Savior.

I pray that God will use this book as an impetus to live before him and may we all "repent and turn to God, and do works worthy of repentance" (Acts 26:20).

Introduction

JOHN WAS REARED IN the home of a dairy farmer. He learned the value of discipline and hard work early in life. He also had a front-row seat to his parents' habitual alcoholism and arguing. John experienced the best and worst of life on the farm. Following in his older brothers' footsteps, John dropped out of high school in search of a different life and "better living," as he explained it.

He left home at age eighteen and was arrested twice by nineteen for drunk and disorderly conduct. In desperate need of a life change, John joined the Marines at age twenty. It was there that John would rediscover the value of self-discipline and gain a sense of pride in serving his country. After basic training, he was deployed to the Mediterranean Sea for six months.

After five months at sea, John was called home due to a severe accident that resulted in his father's premature death. While on emergency leave, John happened to see an old friend: Henry Barns. He farmed with Henry before the Marines. Henry was a Christian and committed to a local church. John could not believe it. "Henry got religion," John thought. This encounter would prove to be pivotal and divine for John.

After completing his tour with the Marines, John returned home and became the family farm's administrator. He soon reconnected with Henry due to their mutual involvement in farm work. It would not take long until Henry invited John to come to church with him. John seriously considered it, mainly because he had tried everything else. So, reluctantly, John finally agreed.

Once John attended church, he desired to keep going back to church with Henry. He attended Bible studies, Sunday school, and worship services. The love and warmth from these people were like nothing he had ever experienced. John was awakened spiritually. Over the weeks and months that ensued, God's word became appealing, and, for the first time he began to understand its meaning. According to John, it was then the emptiness inside him now made sense. He finally knew why he had been so restless and unsatisfied in life.

Then, the most amazing act in John's life occurred. After attending numerous Bible studies and times of worship, during a church service, John surrendered his life to Christ. He repented of his sins and placed his faith and trust in the finished work of the Son of God. As John explained in a personal letter, "It was like the weight of the world was lifted off my shoulders. All that emptiness and void had become satisfied by being replaced with wholeness, completeness, and hope for the future only found in Jesus Christ. The old was passed away, and I was a new person."

John said further that he began living for God instead of himself as he recognized Christ as the Lord of his life. As John recounted, "My life had become filled with joy and purpose for living. I wanted, and continue to desire, to live my life for Christ and bring fame to his name."

This brief snapshot of John's life has painted a portrait for us, a portrait of repentance. In the pages and chapters ahead, it is my goal and desire to lay out for you what repentance means, what repentance looks like, and how to live a life of repentance for the Lord Jesus Christ.

1

What Is Repentance?

J. I. PACKER so poignantly explains, "In the military, nobody doubts what's meant when the order is given, 'Halt! About turn, quick march.' It means that the soldiers are being told to turn their backs on the direction in which they were going and to start marching in the opposite direction from the way they were going before."[1] Repentance. A word that is often neglected in the Christian church. A word that is known by those within and without the church but understood by few. What is repentance, truly? What does this word or, better, concept of repentance really mean?

Repentance can be defined as the activity, or evidence, of being sincerely sorry for your sin. However, with even a cursory reading of the Bible, it is quickly realized that this definition is insufficient. To repent of one's sins is more than just an activity or simply being sorry for wrongdoings. This realization presents a conundrum of sorts, and further begs the question, where does someone find an accurate and complete definition of repentance? Thankfully, there is a place to turn, a book in fact, which provides us with a precise and thorough explanation of repentance. In this book, my primary goal is to begin with and remain with what the Bible and its adherents say about repentance, in prayerful hope

1. Crossway, "What Is Repentance?," 00:00–00:29.

that you and I may know that true repentance resides within our own hearts and lives.

Saint Mark on Repentance

So, how would one answer the question at hand, "What is repentance, truly?" To begin, let us turn our attention to the Gospel of Mark. Mark's narrative concerning the Son of God begins with Christ as an adult, being baptized, tempted by Satan, and beginning his ministry in the very first chapter. The first quotation that this Gospel writer gives us from Jesus are these words from Mark 1:15, "The time is fulfilled, and the kingdom of God is at hand; repent and believe in the gospel."[2] There, in Christ's first recorded proclamation is the word: repent. Not only *in* the sentence, but repent is given as an imperative. In other words, Christ introduces the word "repent" in his preaching as a command, a necessity. Therefore, repentance is not optional, but rather integral to the eternal salvation of the soul.

The word "repent" occurs thirty-four times in the New Testament, twenty-one of which are in the Gospels and the book of Acts. Repentance means to think differently afterwards. In other words, to change one's mind. However, to stop there would not only be too elementary a definition, but it would be to miss the richness and fullness of the meaning of repent in the Gospels and Acts, as well as the rest of the New Testament. A change of the mind may at first seem simple enough, casual even. For example, I am deciding on an ice cream flavor at my favorite ice cream establishment and just as the person filling my request is about to dip that flavor, I suddenly state that I have changed my mind and desire a different flavor. When a person truly contemplates the concept of repentance, its meaning goes much deeper.

To repent is a radical concept. This radical repentance not only involves a change of mind; it is a life-altering turnaround. It is a diversion of location from what displeased God toward a life

2. Every Scripture reference in this book comes from the ESV Bible unless otherwise noted.

that joyfully engages toward a direction that pleases him. In fact, the verses in the first chapter of Mark that immediately follow the words of Christ calling for repentance are the calling of four of his disciples (vv. 16–20). Jesus, going along the shores of Galilee, encounters two sets of brothers, Simon (Peter) and Andrew, and James and John. He calls to each of them, and they immediately leave their nets and follow Christ. James and John leave their vocation, as well as their father, and follow Christ. Notice the gravity of these events in Mark 1:16–20,

> Passing alongside the Sea of Galilee, he saw Simon and Andrew the brother of Simon casting a net into the sea, for they were fishermen. And Jesus said to them, "Follow me, and I will make you become fishers of men." And immediately they left their nets and followed him. And going on a little farther, he saw James the son of Zebedee and John his brother, who were in their boat mending the nets. And immediately he called them, and they left their father Zebedee in the boat with the hired servants and followed him.

Pause and ponder for a moment the implications of what occurs in those verses. The Son of God passes by seasoned fishermen who were not simply catching for sport. Fishing was their livelihood, and more particularly, a family business. It is safe to say that these men grew up knowing that toiling on the waters and shore of the Sea of Galilee would be their place for both employment and enjoyment. As far as these men could tell this was and would be the trajectory of their lives; lives lived out in the fishing business with friends and family alike. However, the Messiah had a different direction for them. The Savior's call was a life-altering call and rearrangement of their businesses and routines. What seemed to be a simple request from a rabbi from Nazareth turned out to be a compelling, irreversible commitment to the Divine, the Son of God.

Mark's placement of the call to discipleship comes at an interesting point in the narrative. These verses directly follow the commanding message of Christ to repent in the preceding verse (15). This order suggests a practical application and outworking of

Jesus's call to repentance. Scripture is not simply revealing the call to repentance, but what it means to repent. Commentator Alan Cole asserts,

> Both pairs of brothers found that obedience to the call of Jesus was costly; it meant abandonment of all that they held dear, and all earthly security, in simple committal to Jesus. Nor can we say that those who left father and hired servants and boat left more than those who left their nets alone, since both left all that they had; that is always the minimum requirement for the Christian. Left and followed correspond to the double call of Jesus in verse 15 "repent and believe."[3]

It is the call to repentance, and the direct application of it, that one begins to apprehend the true sense of the meaning of repentance. In the words of New Testament scholar Robert Stein, "The call to discipleship contains within it a sovereign Christological claim. The present pericope is dominated by Jesus's call to absolute obedience and surrender. From the lips of anyone else, such a totalitarian call is appalling and outrageous, but the one who calls here is not just anyone. He is Jesus Christ, the Son of God."[4]

The resoluteness of repentance is striking. The call of Christ seems simple: "Follow me." Yet, these men's responses were sheer abandonment of all they had known before to what they see now as incomparably better. It is demanding, a bit overwhelming to be sure. The all-encompassing nature of Christ's call is breathtaking. I write this because it seems as if today's call for following Jesus from our pulpits and gospel conversations differs from the call we find from Jesus in the Gospels. For example, the call observed from this first chapter of Mark is one that requires a person's total surrender and submission. This call to repentance is a discombobulating of our priorities until they are rearranged to a God-pleasing and God-delighting way of living.

As you begin to ponder these things, a temptation may arise to be dismissive of a passage such as this one. That is not to say,

3. Cole, *Mark*, 113.
4. Stein, *Mark*, 81.

4

dismissive in the sense that the event and its interpretation are not true, but that it seems non-applicable to the "average Christian." In other words, what is viewed as complete abandonment of career and family on the part of these men surely could not be the template for all Christians going forward, could it? You might ponder, "Did Peter ever fish again?" "How much were James and John a part of their father's life and business after this Christ encounter?" We will return to these kinds of queries, and more, later.

The reason passages of Scripture like this shock us, or even disturb us, is that, too often, we have been peddled a more casual Christianity. We have stripped bare the concept and practice of conversion to two things: making a profession of faith and becoming involved with a local church. There is often no call for repentance, no transformation, and no subsequent reshaping of one's priorities in living. Other than a profession, church attendance, and new friends and acquaintances, life goes on as it did before. The frightening problem with such a Christianity is that it is not Christianity at all. It is at best a pseudo-Christianity, and, at worst, a mockery of what it means to be a Christian that is found in Scripture. This brand of Christianity is simply nowhere to be found in God's word.

In the pages to follow, it is my intention to point you to more biblical portraits of repentance. My desire is for you to observe examples of people authentically displaying a heart, mind, and life transformed by Christ and his gospel. It will be these examples that I hope answer those heart-burning questions concerning true repentance, its implications, and applications.

Thomas Watson on Repentance

Next, let us hear from a figure who can help with incisive insight regarding repentance; one who is quite distant in the past and yet speaks with remarkable precision to the present. The person to whom I am referring to is Thomas Watson, Puritan pastor and author of the seventeenth century. He is known for his fiery preaching and instructive prose, not the least of which is a short work entitled *The Doctrine of Repentance*. In this work, he delivers a poignant and stunning portrait of repentance. For example, Watson asserts, "In Adam we all suffered shipwreck, and repentance is the only plank left us after shipwreck to swim to heaven."[5] Watson clearly views repentance not only as necessary but of critical and primary import. He defines repentance as "a grace of God's Spirit whereby a sinner is inwardly humbled and visibly reformed. Further, repentance is a spiritual medicine made up of six special ingredients: sight of sin, sorrow for sin, confession of sin, shame for sin, hatred for sin, and turning from sin."[6] None of which can be left out.

Watson is thoroughly revealing that sin is severely dealt with when it comes to genuine repentance. He takes each of the above ingredients in his treatise on the matter and perspicuously highlights sin as our problem and turning from it to Christ as our solution. In his own words, "It is not enough to forsake the devil's quarters, but we must get under Christ's banner and wear his colours."[7] This act of turning *from* sin (that which displeases and is an affront to God and his character), and *to* God (living in conjunction with that which pleases God and is in alignment with his character) is the marquee of repentance.

To conclude Watson's thoughts on repentance, I turn to his final words regarding the nature of true repentance. It is here that the Puritan pastor and author provides the marked benefits of repentance to us mere mortals over against the beautiful graciousness of the Divine. He explains,

> Turning to God makes for our profit. Our repentance is of no benefit to God, but to ourselves. If a man drinks of a fountain he benefits himself, not the fountain. If he beholds the lift of the sun, he himself is refreshed by it, not the sun. If we turn from our sins to God, God is not advantaged by it, [but it is us who turn]. If we turn to God, he will turn to us. If God turns to us, all things shall

5. Watson, *Doctrine of Repentance*, 13.

6. Watson, *Doctrine of Repentance*, 18.

7. Watson, *Doctrine of Repentance*, 55.

turn to our good, both mercies and afflictions; we shall taste honey at the end of the rod.[8]

Wow! What an exchange. A truly unbalanced transaction, all in the favor of the one who repents, not to the one who offers it. Jesus certainly paid it all.

J. I. Packer on Repentance

James Innell (J. I.) Packer (1926–2020), English-born, evangelical scholar and theologian, wrote and spoke on the topics of holiness and godliness that must accompany the Christian life which, by logical implication, included copious amounts concerning repentance. Over the many decades of his academic career, Dr. Packer is regarded as one of the most respected conservative evangelical scholars of our day. Therefore, it seems fitting to excise his perspicacity on the matter of repentance.

To begin, Packer provides an encompassing definition of repentance: "Repentance, in the broadest sense, signifies the change of mind, purpose, attitude, and behavior whereby we embrace God's agenda of mercy toward us and turning back from the old life of fighting God by playing God to live the new life of humbly and thankfully serving Him."[9] Notice how Packer gives an all-of-life-encompassing definition of repentance. It is not a mere act of volition or simply a punctiliar event but is much more. In other words, "Repentance is thus a whole-person business in which a pattern of self-centered self-service is replaced by a God-centered habit of seeking others' welfare, and pride and willfulness give way to prayer and worship."[10]

By implication, Packer is pointing out the fact that one's agenda, one's way of living is inappropriate without repentance. More to the point, the trajectory of one's life without Christ is sinful according to God's standards. While this truth may seem obvious,

---

8. Watson, *Doctrine of Repentance*, 58.

9. Packer, *Taking Repentance Seriously*, 7.

10. Packer, *Taking Repentance Seriously*, 7.

it is of fundamental importance that you and I understand our sinfulness. In similar fashion to Watson, Packer points to the issue of sin and one's personal recognition of it to be a clear indication of the rumblings of authentic repentance.

Sin, as one finds in Scripture, expresses the idea of missing some mark, failure to reach a standard, a violation of purity, and/or disobedience to authority. Of course, the mark, the standard, the purity, and the authority are God's. It is God's character and will by which sin is measured. He is the standard by which wayward-ness is noted: "Sin is the deviation from the God who wants our fellowship and worship, and sin embraces self-absorption in place of God-centeredness. To sum up: sin, as a label for our natural state before God, signifies rebellion, defilement, condemnation, and slavery."[11]

In similar fashion, Packer defines repentance as does Watson. Both reflect transformation against the backdrop of God's character and our sinfulness. To give summation to Packer's thoughts on repentance's meaning, note these words: "Repentance, we now see, will always be more than a moment of regret and remorse, plus a word of apology; it will always centre upon turning from and leaving behind what was wrong, and asking God in fullest sincerity to keep us from ever falling back into this wrongness again."[12]

Repentance, then, is a decisive, visible, and seismic shift in a person by both what and whom the person no longer participates, as well as what and who that person now participates. Another perspective is to say that repentance is loving the things of God that one once viewed in apathy or even hatred and hating the things (sin) that one once viewed as both necessary and even ir-resistible. Something this revolutionary must be an act of God. So, journey with me in the pages to come as we see the beautiful, life-changing acts of repentance in the lives of people like you and me.

---

11. Packer, *Taking Repentance Seriously*, 9.
12. Packer, *Taking Repentance Seriously*, 10.

2

What Does Repentance Look Like?

RECALL FROM THE PREVIOUS chapter, Jesus's first recorded message in Mark's Gospel, "The time is fulfilled, and the kingdom of God is at hand; repent and believe in the gospel" (1:15). Jesus's words are not mere suggestions but commands. "Repent and believe" are necessary acts to obtain salvation from one's sins and find shelter in the Savior. The summons to repent and believe in the gospel is sharpened by the mere reality of the one who calls. Jesus, the very Son of God, draws near to mankind and beckons us, "come." Provision has been made, and the time is now: no delay, no postponement. As New Testament scholar Robert Stein explains, "In Jesus men are confronted by the word and act of God; he himself is the crucial term by which belief and unbelief come to fruition. Jesus proclaims the kingdom not to give content but to convey a summons."[1]

It follows, then, that if a person is seeking God, as it were, wanting to be sure of their salvation, or even reexamining their own profession of faith, that one's life would undoubtedly need to be in line with the biblical meaning of the act of repentance. Therefore, you must ask, "What does repentance look like?" That is, not simply from an academic perspective but a personal one. Practically speaking, when Christ bids repent and believe in the gospel,

1. Stein, *Mark*, 74–75.

9

what does he intend for us to do precisely? In this chapter, I want us to glean from two of the reformers, in addition to the apostle Paul, exactly what repentance looks like. The first perspective comes from the face of the protestant reformation, Martin Luther.

Reformation and Repentance: Martin Luther

Luther is quite instructive regarding repentance, in part due to the religious milieu of his day. In large part, Luther's context involved the Roman Catholic Church peddling penance. In other words, the act of repentance had been convoluted by the ambitions of the church. In 1517, Pope Leo X sanctioned indulgences in Germany to fund the construction of St. Peter's Basilica in Rome. Further, these indulgences offered complete forgiveness of past, present, and future sins. With the pope's imprimatur, the indulgence promised absolution of sins without a sign of contrition or genuine repentance. In other words, one could simply buy the forgiveness of sin and right standing with God.[2]

Johann Tetzel, an itinerate Dominican monk, became the papacy's superb salesman. As he entered towns, Tetzel would organize the selling of indulgences to people. These indulgences were sold so that the buyers could receive the church's blessing and promise of forgiveness and righteousness, as well as free their deceased loved ones from the throws of purgatory.[3] Furthermore, Tetzel prepared sermons giving vivid and horrific descriptions of the terrors of purgatory for parish priests to preach before he arrived in their towns.[4] His most famous line was "As soon as the coin in the coffer rings, a soul from purgatory springs."[5]

The indulgences, of course, came at a cost and a particularly acute one to German peasants. In fact, one of Luther's ninety-five arguments points out the burden of the cost of these indulgences.

---

2. Luther, *Martin Luther's Ninety-Five Theses*, 11.
3. Lawson, *Heroic Boldness of Martin Luther*, 8–9.
4. Luther, *Martin Luther's Ninety-Five Theses*, 12.
5. Shelley, *Church History in Plain Language*, 240.

Luther exclaims that if the pope knew this reality, "he would rather that St. Peter's go to ashes than that it should be built up with the skin, flesh, and bones of his sheep."[6] Yet, as Luther later discovers, the Pope not only knew but endorsed this insufferable enterprise.

In this setting, Luther becomes incredibly disturbed and equally moved to combat, in his view, heresy and deception by the church. On October 31, 1517, Luther nails a list of ninety-five statements to the door of the Castle Church in Wittenberg, proposing a public debate concerning the sale of indulgences. These statements became known as the Ninety-Five Theses. Incidentally, Luther's students made copies of this document and distributed these copies throughout the Saxony region. And the rest is history.

The first of his Ninety-Five Theses reveals the impetus for his writing and posting of the infamous document, namely repentance. Luther begins, "When our Lord and Master Jesus Christ said, 'Repent,' he willed the entire life of believers to be one of repentance."[7] Repentance is the focal point of Luther's Theses. Luther employs a number of his theses to provide explicit counterpoints to what had become a heretical view of repentance by the church. Luther is answering the fundamental question: "What is true repentance?"

In a lesser-known work entitled *Explanations of the Disputation Concerning the Value of Indulgences*, Luther provides a thorough discussion of each thesis. Detailing the meaning and implications of the first thesis, Luther writes:

> Nevertheless, I shall prove the thesis for the sake of those who are uninformed, first from the Greek word metanoiei=te itself, which means "repent" and could be translated more exactly by the Latin transmentamini, which means "assume another mind and feeling, recover one's senses, make a transition from one state of mind to another, have a change of spirit. By this recovery of one's senses, it happens that the sinner has a change of heart and hates his sin.[8]

6. Luther, *Martin Luther's Ninety-Five Theses*, 12.

7. Luther, *Martin Luther's Ninety-Five Theses*, 23.

8. Luther, "Explanation of the Ninety-Five Theses," 2.

Luther is aiming to reveal what repentance looks like, its implications, and its effects in the life of the person who embraces it. The repentant life is transformed from the inside out.

One of the significant mantras from the Reformation was a simple, yet profound phrase: *ecclesia reformata, semper reformanda* (the church reformed, always reforming). This cry of the church has often been used as a motto or slogan. However, what may be used as a slogan, is meant for much more. Rather than focusing on the external matters of the church, the phrase is meant to turn our attention to the hearts of the people within the church. It is the transformation of the heart that brings about true reformation. To provide precise and poignant articulation to the matter, carefully read the following from the Canons of Dort under the Third and Fourth Main Points of Doctrine, Article 11,

> When God carries out this good pleasure in the elect, or works true conversion in them, God not only sees to it that the gospel is proclaimed to them outwardly, and enlightens their minds powerfully by the Holy Spirit so that they may rightly understand and discern the things of the Spirit of God, but, by the effective operation of the same regenerating Spirit, God also penetrates into the inmost being, opens the closed heart, softens the hard heart, and circumcises the heart that is uncircumcised. God infuses new qualities into the will, making the dead will alive, the evil one good, the unwilling one willing, and the stubborn one compliant. God activates and strengthens the will so that, like a good tree, it may be enabled to produce the fruits of good deeds.[9]

Luther, and those with similar theological and ecclesiological convictions who followed, had a view of repentance and salvation that encompasses every facet of a person's being, leaves no stone unturned in the crevices of the heart, no priority unarranged, and no life left the same.

---

9. See "Canons of Dort."

Reformation and Repentance: John Calvin

Another pioneer reformer of the sixteenth century who further elucidates the work of repentance is none other than John Calvin. In his systematic theology, *Institutes of the Christian Religion*, Calvin provides a thorough and circumspect perspective regarding repentance. He begins,

> Repentance consists of two parts, mortification and quickening. By mortification I mean, grief of soul and terror, produced by a conviction of sin and a sense of divine judgment. By quickening I mean, the comfort which produced by faith, as when a man prostrated by a consciousness of sin, and smitten with the fear of God, afterward beholding his goodness, and the mercy, grace, and salvation obtained through Christ, looks up, begins to breathe, takes courage, and passes, as it were, from death unto life.[10]

Authentic repentance occurs in the life of a person when, after understanding the gospel, the Holy Spirit convicts the person of their sin, their acts of treason against a holy and righteous God. The Spirit of God breathes life into their deadened soul and produces faith and desire for action, the right action. Therefore, upon the horrifying realization of their state before God, this person, having been awakened from their state of death, steps out of the darkness into his marvelous light.

Calvin goes on to further provide what he calls a "clearer exposition" of the meaning of repentance. He explains, "There are three things to be considered in it: conversion, fear of God, spiritual regeneration."[11] First, the conversion of a life to God requires an intrinsic transformation resulting in external fruit. This metamorphosis occurs because of repentance, "after [the soul] has put off its old habits to bring forth fruits conformable to its renovations."[12] The prophet Ezekiel proclaims to Israel in chapter 18

---

10. Calvin, *Institutes of the Christian Religion*, 386.

11. Calvin, *Institutes of the Christian Religion*, 389.

12. Calvin, *Institutes of the Christian Religion*, 389.

that repentance comes with the making of a "new heart and a new spirit" (18:31). The apostle Paul reflects in his second letter to the Corinthians that one's union with Christ results in a "new creation" (5:17). It is not, therefore, a working from the outside inward, but an eradication of impiety from the innermost part of the heart that works out to beautiful acts of works and worship in the life of the repentant.

Second, is that "repentance proceeds from a sincere fear of God."[13] When Scripture calls for repentance, it often introduces the subject of judgment. For example, in Acts 17:30–31, "The times of ignorance God overlooked, but now He commands all people everywhere to repent because he has fixed a day on which he will judge the world in righteousness by a man whom he has appointed; and of this, he has given assurance to all by raising him from the dead." The good news of the gospel is most clearly elucidated and magnified when placed against the black backdrop of our sin and the coming just wrath of God.

The third and final piece of Calvin's picture of repentance is spiritual regeneration. It is important to note at the outset of this discussion that he is not referring to the punctiliar act of regeneration, that moment in which one is born again. Instead, Calvin is referring to the Holy Spirit's instilling holiness into our souls, inspiring us with new thoughts and affections, so that we may put off the old man, and be renewed in the spirit of our mind.[14] It is here that Calvin is describing the progressive sanctification that occurs in the life of the follower of Christ as they pursue him with the practice of ongoing repentance. As he concludes, "the nearer anyone approaches in resemblance to God, the more does the image of God appear in him. God assigns repentance as the goal toward which they must keep running during the whole course of their lives."[15] More on this in chapter 4.

---

13. Calvin, *Institutes of the Christian Religion*, 389.

14. Calvin, *Institutes of the Christian Religion*, 390.

15. Calvin, *Institutes of the Christian Religion*, 391.

Godly Grief vs Worldly Sorrow:
The Apostle Paul Regarding Repentance

Now let us turn to the apostle Paul who provides further insight into the workings of repentance. In his second letter to the Corinthians, Paul provides vivid lucidity on the topic. The great apostle opens a window to better view the landscape of authentic repentance. The occasion of the following passage in 2 Corinthians is an offense committed by some of the believers in Corinth against the apostle, his reaction to the offense, and more importantly, the Corinthians' response. The most poignant part of this passage is found in 2 Cor 7:9–11:

> As it is, I rejoice, not because you were grieved, but because you were grieved into repenting. For you felt a godly grief, so that you suffered no loss through us. For godly grief produces a repentance that leads to salvation without regret, whereas worldly grief produces death. For see what earnestness this godly grief has produced in you, but also what eagerness to clear yourselves, what indignation, what fear, what longing, what zeal, what punishment! At every point you have proved yourselves innocent in the matter.

In these few verses, we discover a remarkable distinction between genuine repentance and nothing more than remorse and regret. For context, the apostle had previously written a scathing rebuke that caused the Corinthians incessant sorrow, but sorrow that led to their repentance. He rejoices in that reality and then contrasts worldly and godly grief. Not all grief is the same. Let us consider each of these in turn.

First, worldly grief. Worldly grief is mere regret. Offenders demonstrate regret for what they have done because they have been caught or feel shame. Worldly grief is deficient in God's economy. It is an expression of regret over "opportunities lost, painful present circumstances, or personal embarrassment."[16] Further, pastor and commentator Kent Hughes explains, "Worldly

---

16. DeYoung, "Worldly Grief," para. 4.

grief is a grief for oneself, centered on self, not grief for sin against God. It grieves over consequences. It aches with embarrassment. It focuses on its own hurt and is self-pitying."[17] Sorrow in and of itself is not enough. Emotion without effect, grief without gears is powerless to transform.

Worldly sorrow lacks a vertical dimension. It does not allow us to see our sin and offense against God. Pastor and author Kevin DeYoung rightly notes, "Worldly grief is owing to one of two causes: losing something dear to us or the negative opinion of others."[18] As a result of worldly grief, the focus tends to remain on self and how to "fix" the problem that is causing the daunting guilt or grief. Sin, in worldly grief, is ultimately not dealt with by the cause but merely the symptoms. Truth be told, the heart would rather remain in sin rather than make the effort of seeking reconciliation and true lasting change. In the end, worldly grief leaves us in the throes of the past or focused on the consequences of the present instead of seeking reconciliation with a holy God, falling onto the mercies of the Savior.

The selfishness of worldly grief gives rise to despair, bitterness, and even paralysis.[19] Worldly grief makes you idle and stagnant. You do not change. You do not grow. Two biblical examples come to mind that demonstrate the act and end of worldly sorrow. Esau, although displaying bitter and intense sorrow, grieved, not over any wrongdoing, but over selling his own birthright and the personal loss he incurred (Heb 12:17). Judas, overcome with grief by his betrayal of Christ, turned to despair not the divine, and took his own life as a result (Matt 27). The sad, but clear end of worldly grief is death of the worst kind, namely spiritual.

On the other hand, godly grief leads to repentance; a change of mind and heart, as well as a willingness to act, to change one's behavior empowered by the Spirit of God. Godly sorrow motivates us to go to God, and our salvation takes root in it. New Testament commentator Colin Kruse asserts, "Repentance itself is not the

---

17. Hughes, *2 Corinthians: Power in Weakness*, 151.

18. DeYoung, "Worldly Grief," para. 5.

19. Garland, *2 Corinthians*, 250.

cause of salvation; rather, God saves us and freely forgives our sins only when our repentance shows that we have renounced them."[20] This sorrow over sin "incites us to seek to do something about the problem by taking the past tense and allowing God to turn it into his future tense."[21]

In fact, the apostle provides seven pieces of evidence regarding the authenticity of the Corinthians' repentance: earnestness, eagerness, indignation, fear, longing, zeal, and punishment. Godly grief has worked a full-orbed, dynamic repentance. These evidences, these descriptors, reveal a seriousness to deal with sin, a purposeful intention to turn away from wrongdoing, to get right with God, and to stay right with him. Godly grief, leading to repentance, mobilizes a person to action, "to change, to make right our wrongs, to be zealous for good works, to run from sin and start walking in the opposite direction."[22]

Positively, the earnestness of a repentant sinner is one who seeks to do away with indifference and apathy and become intentionally serious about how he or she lives. This earnestness to live a godly life is coupled with eagerness. It is not simply an obligation to turn away from sin and walk Godward, but it is a joyful obligation and a pleasurable journey. Living the Christian life is not viewed as a list of "dos and don'ts" but as a beautiful pilgrimage toward eternal bliss with the One who turned you in the right direction.

Negatively, authentic repentance produces indignation toward sin. This kind of repentance creates a deep-seated disgust of the thoughts, intentions, and actions that disgust God and are known to displease him, refuse him, and ignore his authority and created order. Pastor and author Tim Keller further explains, "Repentance out of conviction over mercy is really sorrow over sin, sorrow over the grievousness of sin—it melts the heart away from sin. It makes the sin itself disgusting to us, so it loses its attractive power over us."[23] Further, authentic repentance is evidenced by

20. Kruse, 2 Corinthians, 192.

21. Garland, 2 Corinthians, 251.

22. DeYoung, "Godly Grief," para. 8.

23. Keller and Thompson, Church Planter Manual, 39.

a healthy fear of God. Solomon instructs us in Proverbs that the beginning of wisdom, godly wisdom, is the fear of the LORD (Prov 9:10). Genuine repentance is revealed, in part, by living in reverential awe of God such that your life's priorities are rearranged. You strive to stop doing the things that displease God, namely sin. In turn, you purpose to do the things that God commands, that God delights in you doing (Dan 1:8).

Therefore, a question to consider: what is the significance of godly grief leading to repentance? This repentance leads to salvation with no regrets. It is living a life that seeks to please the one who died to grant us both life transformation and life eternal. In Jesus, a person is confronted by the word of God. In Jesus, we are called to a radical decision. A decision, when made in the affirmative, that results in unspeakable joy and a life that is abundant and worth living. As a follower of Jesus lives a life of repentance, he finds himself enraptured by the beauty of God's kingdom of which he now is a part, the work of God's kingdom of which he now participates, and when he reaches the finish line of this life, the breathtaking wonder of his faith made sight.

3

Portraits of Repentance

It is said, "a picture is worth a thousand words." Quite often a picture, a visual, an image conveys to the mind an idea more quickly and effectively than the written word. A photograph, artwork, drawing, or graphics often demonstrate an idea with one look, more quickly than a narrative can explain things. Portraits depict emotion, enabling the viewer to perceive the essence of the story without a word being written or spoken. The slogan seems to have first been put forth around the turn of the twentieth century by a newspaper editor Tess Flanders, discussing strategies in publishing, editing and news reporting. The phrase was popularized in the 1920s by Fred R. Barnard, who is often credited with the origin of the proverb. He used the phrase "a picture is worth a thousand words" to discuss the use of drawn and photographic images to illustrate advertising.[1]

The goal of this chapter is to paint portraits (with words, ironically) of repentance. The hope is that these portraits provide greater insight into what it looks like when a person encounters the truth of the gospel and repents. More specifically, Luke is to be our painter, our art docent as it were. We are going to come alongside the journeys of the rich young ruler and his counterpart

1. Stevenson, *Macmillan Book of Proverbs*.

Zacchaeus from Luke's Gospel, as well as Cornelius and Lydia, both from Luke's recording in the Acts of the Apostles. These biblical characters will provide the rich and meaningful essence of the act and process of repentance. As we gaze on these figures together, the anticipation and expectation are that we too have found, or if not, will find, authentic repentance to be a part of our own experience as confessing Christ followers.

Luke's Arrangement of Repentance: The Rich Young Ruler and Zacchaeus

The Synoptic Gospels (Matthew, Mark, Luke) record a ruler's encounter with Jesus. All three Gospels describe this person as rich. Matthew states he is a young man, and Luke calls him a "certain ruler." Ruler here is a reference to a "ruler of the synagogue" (Luke 8:41) or possibly a member of the Sanhedrin (23:13; 24:20). The rich young ruler is important to our look at repentance because of his response to Christ as well as the arrangement and contrast Luke paints with this rich young ruler over against the backdrop of another influential and wealthy character. Sometimes it is instructive to understand what something is by identifying what it is not. Here in Luke's account, he arranges two events, two people, in such a way that reveals first what repentance is not, and second, what repentance truly is.

The Rich Young Ruler

The rich young ruler approaches Jesus and he asks an insightful and eternally significant question: "Good Teacher, what must I do to inherit eternal life?" Given the context of Luke 18, the ruler had listened and observed Jesus's teaching and actions, and found them intriguing, if not compelling. Therefore, his question is a genuine one. However, as pastor and commentator Kent Hughes describes, "there is a subtle negative here, because the ruler's question assumed that he had the inner power to do whatever was required and that he was intrinsically good."[2] Furthermore, in his estimation he had what it takes to become a Christ follower, and further, that repentance was not a necessary ingredient.

Rather than answering his question directly, Jesus asked a question in return: "Why do you call me good?" Jesus is probing the young ruler's understanding of what it means to be good. Interestingly, there is not one example in the Talmud of a rabbi being addressed as "good."[3] If no one is objectively good except God alone, and this inquisitive young ruler ascribes good to Jesus and his ministry, he would be confessing that the kingdom of God is at hand. Recall what John the Baptizer and Christ himself had preached from the beginning: "Repent, for the kingdom of God is at hand" (Matt 3:2; 4:17; Mark 1:15). Therefore, if the kingdom of God is at hand, and one must repent, then it follows that this young ruler will be called upon by Christ to repent.

Now, Christ's focus turns to the insufficient goodness of the ruler. He did so by pointing him to the law, namely the latter half of the Ten Commandments. The young ruler's response? He replies, "All these I have kept from my youth?" First, you must think, no way you have kept these commandments. You have never stolen anything? Never lied? Never dishonored your parents? More than that, however, is Jesus's response to how the rich young ruler viewed himself, his spiritual condition. Jesus asserts, "One thing you still lack. Sell all that you have and distribute to the poor, and you will have treasure in heaven; and come, follow me." This statement strikes at the very heart of this man's true spiritual state.

Jesus points out to this rich young ruler the reality that resides in each of our hearts. The reality that, without Christ, we worship and trust in something or someone other than God. In his case, the rich young ruler was trusting in his wealth. The rich man loved his possessions more than he loved God. He trusted in what he had accrued and achieved over and above the God who had provided his allowances. Jesus went after the one thing that was the rich ruler's problem, and when Christ revealed it, the young man knew

2. Hughes, *Luke*, 637.
3. Morris, *Luke*, 292.

it.[4] His response? Luke tells us, "But when he heard these things, he became very sad, for he was extremely rich." More poignantly, Mark's Gospel declares, "Disheartened by the saying, he went away sorrowful, for he had great possessions" (10:22). How sad! He appeared so close to the kingdom of God, yet so far away.

Amy Carmichael, missionary to India, writes of a conversation she once had with a Hindu queen in which she pressed Ms. Carmichael to explain to her what was necessary for salvation. With reticence at first, she began to explain. The queen's determination and insistence to hear the full truth regarding salvation in Christ led Amy to fully divulge. She recalls,

> She knew quite enough to understand and take in the force of the forceful words. She would not consent to be led gently on. "No, I must know it now," she said; and as verse by verse we read to her, her face settled sorrowfully. "So far must I follow, so far?" she said, "I cannot follow so far."[5]

In essence, the Hindu queen and the rich young ruler came to the same conclusion: "I cannot follow so far." What Christ was calling on the rich young ruler to do is *repent*. What Amy Carmichael was calling on the Hindu queen to do is *repent*. What Christ is calling on you and me to do is *repent*. As theologian and martyr Dietrich Bonhoeffer, referring to the cross and call of Christ, asserts, "When Christ calls a man, he bids him come and die."[6] The rich young ruler could not, would not, repent. What about you?

Zacchaeus

Now that we have encountered what repentance is not, let us turn our attention towards the opposite direction. Again, note the arrangement of Luke's accounts of repentance or the lack thereof. Just a few verses away, in the very next chapter of Luke (19:1–10),

4. Hughes, *Luke*, 639.
5. Carmichael, *Things as They Are*, 74.
6. Bonhoeffer, *Cost of Discipleship*, 99.

the third Gospel provides a direct contrast to the rich young ruler, namely Zacchaeus. Here is a chief Jewish tax collector, quite possibly one of the most despised persons of his day. Yet, like the rich young ruler, Zacchaeus has an odd curiosity towards Jesus. Luke records that "he was seeking to see who Jesus was." So much so, as Christ comes his way, because of the crowd and his small stature, he climbs up a sycamore tree just to see the Lord pass. As Jesus comes by his way, he calls Zacchaeus to himself. Jesus said to him, "Zacchaeus, hurry and come down, for I must stay at your house today" (Luke 19:5).

As you read the Bible, such as the passage before us, it is easy to overlook certain phrases that prove to be extremely critical to understanding a text of Scripture. Ponder this for a moment: the Lord of the universe is in the very place of this one man, and he summons Zacchaeus. His response? "So he hurried and came down and received him joyfully" (Luke 19:6). At that moment, something happened in the heart and life of this chief tax collector, and we see it in the words that follow.

Zacchaeus invites Jesus to his house as his guest of honor. He confesses and commits to Christ that he is giving away half of his belongings (not earnings) to those who are in true need of them. Further, he proclaims that he is righting those he has financially cheated by repaying them back four times the amount they are owed. Scripture reveals the fruit consistent with repentance (Luke 3:8). That is not to say that the change of behavior is itself repentance, but it demonstrates a change of heart has taken place. Repentance is inextricably linked to obedience.

If we are not convinced of Zacchaeus's conversion, Jesus leaves no room for doubt at the conclusion of this passage: "Today salvation has come to this house, since he also is a son of Abraham. For the Son of Man came to seek and to save the lost" (Luke 19:9–10). It is in this precise moment that Christ, in Luke's account, chooses to use what transpired with this man Zacchaeus to illustrate for us both what repentance means and how repentance works out in a person's life who has been transformed by the power of the gospel.

Counting the Cost

Luke provides a beautiful and arresting contrast between the rich young ruler and the chief tax collector. One perceives the treasures he has accumulated to be invaluable, impossible to relinquish, and the other sees Christ as the treasure of all treasures, the pearl of great price. As Jon Bloom explains in his article "The Cost of Nondiscipleship":

> Two men both encountered Jesus. One was unwilling to lose his possessions; the other was unwilling to keep them. What made the difference? The thing they each treasured most. They each counted the cost and made their choice. Jesus tells us to count the cost of discipleship (Luke 14:26–33). But if we count the cost primarily in terms of what we will lose on earth, we're focusing on the wrong cost. Jesus wants us to count the cost of nondiscipleship: "For what will it profit a man if he gains the whole world and forfeits his soul?" (Matthew 16:26).[7]

Although no explicit demand for repentance is recorded in these passages, it is certainly implicit. Recall Jesus's words in Luke 5:32—"I have not come to call the righteous but sinners to repentance." These men, who are clearly sinners, are called to repent. One does not and one does. The rich young ruler walks away sad, denying Jesus and rejecting the call to repent. Zacchaeus illustrates for us the bearing of fruits in keeping with repentance (Luke 3:8). Christ does not command Zacchaeus to give away half his possessions and make things right fourfold with those he has usuriously robbed, and yet he does. It is not the transformative behavior that is repentance, rather it is the evidence of it. Repentance is more than a change of external behavior, but it is certainly not less. That is the portrait of Zacchaeus; does it resemble yours?

7. Bloom, "Cost of Nondiscipleship," paras. 10–11.

Acts of Repentance

In the book of Acts, Luke continues where he left off in his Gospel. Recall Acts 1:1–3—"In the first book, O Theophilus, I have dealt with all that Jesus began to do and teach, until the day when he was taken up, after he had given commands through the Holy Spirit to the apostles whom he had chosen. He presented himself alive to them after his suffering by many proofs, appearing to them during forty days and speaking about the kingdom of God." Writing to the same person, Luke's authorial intent is to give an orderly account of the church after Christ's resurrection to undergird the certainty of what had been taught (see Luke 1:3–4). More to the point at hand, Luke continues to display for us beautiful, meaningful, and rich acts of repentance by those who encounter the gospel of Christ as it is spread from Jerusalem to the ends of the earth (Acts 1:8). In the paragraphs that follow, we will focus our attention on two such acts, namely the stories of Cornelius and Lydia.

Cornelius

In chapter 10 of Acts, we find the account of Cornelius and Peter. It is, quite possibly, one of the most important passages in the book of Acts. It is the first recorded instance of the gospel being proclaimed directly to a gentile and his household.[8] It is a fascinating orchestration by the providence and sovereignty of God to provide further confirmation that Jesus came into the world to save sinners (1 Tim 1:15). Let us begin with the background and context of Acts 10.

Cornelius is a centurion, a respected man of Caesarea. He is one of the commanders of the Italian cohort of the Roman army, commanding one hundred men within a six-hundred-member unit. Luke describes Cornelius in four positive descriptions. Cornelius is devout, fears God, generous, and prays often (10:2).[9] What

8. Bock, *Luke.*
9. Bock, *Luke.*

ensues is the confluence of two unlikely people and cultures, as well as the juxtaposition of a religion and a relationship (vv. 1–2).

During his daily prayers, Cornelius has a vision of an angel who confirms the effectiveness of his prayers and that he is to send men to find Simon who is called Peter. The angel further tells Cornelius where to find Peter. He obeys the words of the angel, explains to the men to be sent out exactly what had taken place, and sends them to Joppa, approximately thirty miles away, to find this man called Peter (vv. 3–8).

The next day, as these men are traveling to Joppa, Peter goes up on the housetop to pray. Here, he has a vision of something like a sheet coming down in front of him and having diverse kinds of animals on it which are considered unclean to the orthodox Jew. A voice tells him to kill and eat the animals, which Peter refuses. His reasoning is that he has never eaten anything common or unclean. This occurs three times, with the critical comment, "What God has made clean, do not call common" (v. 15). After the three occurrences, the *sheet* was taken up at once to heaven (vv. 9–16).

While Peter is perplexed, pondering what just occurred, the three men sent by Cornelius show up at the door of the house in which Peter is lodging. The Holy Spirit relays to him that these men have arrived and that he is to go with them without hesitation. The men explain their reason for coming, and so Peter invites them in to be his guests (vv. 17–23).

The next day, Peter and his companions go with the men back to Cornelius's place. Cornelius is waiting expectantly. Upon entering, Peter explains who he is and how it is unlawful for him, a Jew, to enter the house of a gentile. This moment is noteworthy, and yet easily overlooked. It is a forbidden act for Peter to enter the home of a gentile. According to the Jewish customs of the day, it is not the contact with gentiles, but primarily any impure foods that may be offered at the table. Therefore, it was understood that Jews and gentiles did not comingle, as a practice. Nevertheless, Peter obeyed, without hesitation, the voice of the Lord telling him to not call anything common or unclean that he had made clean and to go with the men to Cornelius's home (vv. 24–29).

This account is a critical juncture and one that the Holy Spirit is going to enlighten both Peter and Cornelius of the reality that salvation belongs to the Lord. As a result, Scripture reveals that Cornelius relays with laser-focused precision what God had orchestrated to bring Peter and the gospel message to him and his household. More than that, Cornelius explains that he and all his family have come together to listen to Peter proclaim what the Lord had given to him. It is here that Peter confesses, for the first time, he truly understands that God shows no partiality (vv. 30–35).

Peter begins to proclaim to Cornelius and his household the good news of the gospel. "The central part of which explains the significance of Jesus's person and ministry in three parts: God's fulfillment of his promise of salvation for all people through Jesus (v. 36), Jesus's ministry of proclamation and healing (vv. 37–39c), and Jesus's death and resurrection (vv. 39d–41)."[10] God sent his word to Israel and now to the gentiles preaching peace through Jesus Christ because God keeps his promises and he is Lord of all. Peter then reminds them of the life and public ministry of Jesus: doing good and healing people, for God was with him. Peter is emphasizing the reality that Jesus is God's anointed, and that God has endowed him with the Holy Spirit and power.

He preaches Christ, his death on the cross and resurrection. He then assures his audience of the veracity of his witness, that he personally saw Christ do these things as well as providing incontrovertible evidence of his resurrection. Peter concludes with the Great Commandment, the mandate to preach this good news to everyone and to warn them of the judgement of God as well as the forgiveness of sins available for everyone who believes in and through the name of Jesus. Because he is Lord of all, Christ has the power and authority to both judge the world and offer full pardon and forgiveness of the sins that bring judgement. In summary, Peter preached the message of the gospel to these gentiles (vv. 42–43).

While he was preaching, the Holy Spirit came upon Cornelius and his household. The presence of the triune God was manifested

10. Schnabel, *Acts*, 502.

as a sign, authenticating the effect of the gospel and conversion of these people. Peter recognizes this reality and calls for their baptism as an external act symbolizing their internal transformation. This act confirms that what God makes clean is clean indeed. These gentiles have come to faith in Christ and received the Spirit of God just as the Jews had. Furthermore, they asked Peter to stay a few days afterward, as an act of kindness and an opportunity to spread the gospel of Christ (vv. 44–48).

There are two key realities worth noting from this passage. One is the fact that Cornelius is described as a devout, God-fearing, generous, and prayerful person. These qualities alone are not enough in the economy of God to render Cornelius righteous or justified before the Lord. New Testament Darrell Bock describes Cornelius initially: "He was respectful of God but had not yet responded to Jesus."[11] The reality is that Cornelius and his household needed to hear the gospel, needed to repent, and needed to believe in Christ alone for their salvation. Being religious is not enough. The second reality is the supernatural work of God. Peter is sent for this reason. Note Peter's message. It is simple, straightforward, not earth-shattering in the sense we rank sermons nowadays. What was the difference? The Holy Spirit manifested in such a way to bring blinded eyes sight, sinful people to repentance and faith, and a turning to Christ as Savior and Lord. That is the difference.

Repentance Recognized

While reading and recalling the events of Acts 10, you might wonder, is that repentance I just read about? How do we know that is an act of repentance by Cornelius and his household? These are good questions, but first, let us address the response from the early church headquarters in Jerusalem.

As Acts 11 begins, news has spread throughout the region of gentiles receiving the word of God. This message reveals an interesting and significant perspective of equivocating the conversion

---

11. Bock, *Acts*, 402.

of Cornelius and his household to receiving God's word. This declaration validates that the proclamation of the word of God is crucial when presenting the gospel.

Here, Scripture reveals that Peter is headed back to Jerusalem, the early church's "headquarters." He has come, in part, to report on the amazing and divinely appointed events that have occurred in the region of Caesarea. It is important to note that the Jewish church leaders will, at first, see the spread of the gospel to gentiles as disingenuous on Peter's part, even scandalous. As commentator Darrel Bock asserts, "There is little question that the church would have found such a revolutionary move initially controversial, which would require a defense of its legitimacy and a justification for this new avenue of ministry."[12] As verses 2–3 reveal, Peter is met with criticism for sharing a meal in the home of a gentile. Therefore, Peter begins immediately providing the evidence of God's salvation spreading beyond the Jewish people.

Peter begins his explanation, recalling his vision and detailing the events leading up to his visit to Cornelius's household (vv. 5–14). At this point, while riveting, and as you might imagine, all are hanging on his every word, Peter comes to the most important portion of his account. He says in verses 15 and 16, "As I began to speak, the Holy Spirit fell on them just as on us at the beginning. And I remembered the word of the Lord, how he said, 'John baptized with water, but you will be baptized with the Holy Spirit.'" This proclamation is the linchpin moment of a new era. In this occasion, the Lord demonstrated that the gentiles are also a part of the plan of salvation.

Peter's conclusion: "Who was I that I could stand in God's way?" (v. 17b). When the Holy Spirit does such a work, nothing or no one can stand in his way. We have the privilege of hindsight, noting the divinely orchestrated appointments to see that Cornelius and his household came to trust Jesus Christ as Savior and Lord. However, in the moment, how will the early church leaders respond? Verse 18 reveals their response. They glorified God!

12. Bock, *Acts*, 405.

Their responses were ones of praise and honor, lifting up the One who is responsible for the salvation of gentiles.

Now back to the question I asked earlier, "How do we know that is an act of repentance by Cornelius and his household?" Interestingly, the answer comes from the Jewish church leaders. They abandoned their objections and exclaimed, "Then to the Gentiles also God has granted repentance that leads to life" (Acts 11:18). What a significant statement. Note each portion of the latter half of that statement—"God has granted repentance that leads to life." God, in Christ, initiated the divine appointment of Peter and Cornelius, the cultivation of their hearts to be able to both give (Peter) the gospel and receive (Cornelius and his household) the gospel, and life eternal by and through the Holy Spirit as a result. In other words, God took the initiative that resulted in repentance as the response and life as the gift.[13]

If you were not convinced that Cornelius and his household is another portrait of God's grace in granting repentance, then the Jewish leaders in Acts 11 have helped to remove any doubt. From a human perspective, this is often the unanticipated expectation of the Lord. Think about this reality: that God would come along in time and choose someone like Cornelius, like us, mere sinners, to be a part of his kingdom, and, in a broader sense, the amazing reality that Christ gave himself on a cross to die for our sins, in the place that we deserve, to save us, to make us his own. Further, that we, in turn, would turn to him in response and trust him to be who he says he is: Savior and Lord, protector, provider, the eternal and perfect God. What a marvelous picture of his sovereignty and divine orchestration to remove cultural barriers, soften hearts, intersect lives, save sinners.

Lydia

It is against that backdrop we come to the next portrait in the gallery of repentance. In Acts 16 Luke provides yet another beautiful

---

13. Bock, *Acts*, 409.

account found situated in the principal city of Philippi in Macedonia. The Lord, in his sovereign plan, brought Paul and his companions to this region to spread the good news of Jesus Christ. After staying there for a few days, on the Sabbath, the apostle Paul and his company travel just outside the city to the riverside where a number of women are gathered at a place of prayer. One of the ladies there was named Lydia. Scripture describes her as a seller of purple goods, which is an indicator that she was a lady of means. She is also described as a God-fearer or worshiper of God, usually indicating a polytheistic adherent converted to monotheism, becoming a worshiper of the God of Israel.

However, like Cornelius, being devout and one who feared God is not enough. The apostle Paul comes to this location to engage in gospel conversation and to preach the reality of Jesus Christ as Savior and Lord. While Paul is preaching, Scripture tells us that Lydia listened with her heart. Notice the key phrase in the second half of Acts 16:14, "The Lord opened her heart to pay attention to what was said by Paul." As with Cornelius, it was a divine initiation that caused Lydia to truly listen, not just with her ears but her heart. This is important because, as the apostle Paul puts it in Rom 10, it is "with the heart one believes and is justified" (10:10a). It is not simply intellectual assent that saves a person. It is a supernatural event. As New Testament scholar Eckhard Schnabel asserts,

> Paul spoke, Lydia listened, but it was the Lord who "opened" Lydia's heart, causing her to understand and accept the gospel. On account of the Lord's initiative, Lydia "followed" closely the words spoken by Paul and turned to the proclamation of the good news of Jesus, Israel's Messiah, whose death, resurrection, and exaltation provides for the forgiveness of sins and eternal life to those who put their trust in Jesus.[14]

Luke, inspired by the Holy Spirit, reveals to his readers yet another perspective on repentance. God initiates the call of the gospel by sending Paul to the banks of the river outside Philippi

14. Schnabel, *Acts*, 681.

where he proclaims the gospel, the Lord opened Lydia's heart to listen closely, and she believed. The evidence of her conversion, her repentance, is threefold. One, she is baptized (and her household believed and was baptized) as a public profession of her faith in Christ. Two, she displays humility, insistent hospitality, and generosity by opening her home to the apostle Paul and his company. It is later discovered (v. 40) that Lydia's home becomes the birthplace of the church at Philippi. Third is the acceptance of her invitation by the apostle Paul, rendering an affirmation that she had been judged faithful to the Lord (v. 15b).

Do You See What I See?

After careful consideration and examination, my prayer is that you see in these portraits the reality of repentance. When a person encounters Christ, that person is never the same. There is a transformation that is only explained by including divine intervention in the explanation. To be more precise, it is God, in his mercy and grace, sending his Son for his own to seek and to save the lost, that is the ultimate act of divine intervention. So that, in response, by his granting, we may turn in repentance away from our lifestyle of sin to a lifestyle of godly living. More than this, his intervention allows us to see Christ as our greatest treasure, our fondest possession. It is the gift of eternal life. The life-giving Spirit of God is the divine provision. The role of the Spirit as life-giver is the link between the gift and the possession of that gift. In other words, he is the link between our salvation and our sanctification as repentant Christ followers. Which, therefore, begs the question: what does repentance look like in the life of a believer? I endeavor to answer this question in the next chapter.

4

Repentance in the
Life of the Believer

LUKE RECORDS THIS JARRING assertion at the end of chapter 9 of his Gospel: "Jesus said to him, 'No one who puts his hand to the plow and looks back is fit for the kingdom of God.'" What a powerful and captivating declaration. Jesus is poignantly declaring to his listeners the cost of discipleship. That a person who turns to follow Christ may not turn back from following him, or they are not a genuine disciple is a proclamation simultaneously understandable and frightening. In this chapter, my intention is to answer the question, "What does a 'no turning back' repentance look like in the life of a Christ follower?"

The contemporary use of the word *repentance* is often limited to conversion, the event of regeneration, when an unbeliever turns and becomes a believer, a Christ follower. Yet, recall that repentance is not just regretful remorse, but "a total about-turn in one's thoughts, aims, and acts, so that one leaves the paths of self-willed disobedience to serve God in faith and faithfulness."[1] Of course, a person does not follow the path of obedience and faithfulness in full measure for the rest of their lives. However, striving to stay on

1. Packer, *Growing in Christ*, 124.

the path of godliness is evidence that you have been placed on that path in the first place. The Christian life is one of repeated reorientations. As J. I. Packer explains in his book *Growing in Christ*,

> What is crucial, however, is that the marks of conversion—faith and repentance as principles of daily living—should be found in us; otherwise, we cannot be judged Christians at all, whatever experiences we may claim. Thus, the converted lifestyle is more significant than any conversion experience.[2]

The remarkable evidence of authentic repentance is that a person keeps on repenting. It is the lifestyle of the converted that gives away the genuineness of their conversion experience. This evidence marks a person as to whether they are a true Christ follower.

Now, returning to Luke, who echoes the truth of repentance in his Gospel, as well as offering an insightful perspective on grasping the evidence of authentic repentance. Recall in Luke chapter 3, John the Baptist, the herald of Christ, is preaching to the crowd and charging those who came to him to not trust their cultural or religious heritage, but to make a personal response to God. Specifically, see the first half of verse 8: "bear fruits in keeping with repentance." This phrase is crucial for understanding the effects of authentic repentance. Think about it—fruit originates from something. It is the effect or result of something else. Repentance is an internal change of heart and mind that reorients a person's way of living, inevitably resulting in godly obedience.

Stating it more bluntly, David Wells asserts, "The only real proof of our conversion is an obedient and fruitful life."[3] The apostle Paul, while witnessing to King Agrippa, describes his preaching the gospel, in part, by saying "that they should repent and turn to God, performing deeds in keeping with their repentance" (Acts 26:20). By his testimony, Paul is confirming that the logical progression of hearing and believing the gospel is to turn to God in repentance, and then live in such a way that your habits,

---

2. Packer, *Growing in Christ*, 124.

3. Wells, *Turning to God*, 40.

your deeds, the bent of your life is in alignment with one who has repented. Conversely, the one who claims repentance and yet does not perform deeds in keeping with their repentance may have not repented in the first place.

Again, this phrase from Luke, "bear fruits in keeping with repentance," evokes burning questions such as: What are the fruits of repentance? What are the practices and the disciplines by which a repentant believer lives? If this command comes to all who repent, how does that look in the life of a disciple of Christ? Throughout the New Testament, the term *fruit* or *fruits* is most often used metaphorically to indicate the visible expression or evidence of what has occurred internally and invisibly in the life of a follower of Jesus. The word *fruit* in Scripture often means the practices or characteristics displayed while living the Christian life. Using the term *practice* as a synonym for *fruit*, the following pages present five practices effectuated in the life of a believer who has genuinely repented. As you work your way through each of these practices, note that they are logically and progressively linked, and work in a cyclical fashion throughout the Christian life.

Confronting Sin

One of the first and primary practices that comes from authentic repentance is the practice of confronting sin. As followers of Christ, it is both an awareness of the reality of being redeemed, and yet living with sin. As Paul reminds us in Rom 7, "So I find it to be a law that when I want to do right, evil lies close at hand. For I delight in the law of God, in my inner being, but I see in my members another law waging war against the law of my mind and making me captive to the law of sin that dwells in my members. Wretched man that I am! Who will deliver me from this body of death?"

Given the reality of this struggle, this spiritual war, how do followers of Jesus confront sin? First, rather than ignoring or relenting to the reality of the presence of sin, we must face our sin and act. The first act is to stand in the shadow of the cross. Pastor and author Tim Keller explains, "Christians think that we are saved by the gospel, but then we grow by applying biblical principles to every area of life. But we are not just saved by the gospel, we grow by applying the gospel to every area of life."[4] He further elaborates to assert that "the root of all our disobedience is particular ways in which we continue to seek control of our lives through systems of works-righteousness."[5]

Further, Christians, must ensure their lives are in line with the gospel. Believers must be creatures of the word of God, saturating our minds and hearts in the Scriptures. Leaning again on Keller's insight, "The way to progress as a Christian is continually to repent and uproot these systems (systems of sinful behavior) in the same way that we became Christians—by the vivid depiction of Christ's saving work for us, and the abandoning of self-trusting efforts to complete ourselves."[6] There it is, continual repentance. As Kevin DeYoung observes,

> Few things are more important than repentance. No doubt, the church is for broken and imperfect people— broken people who hate what is broken in them and imperfect people who have renounced their sinful imperfections. [Therefore, we are] to labor for a church community where lifelong repentance is the normal experience of Christian discipleship.[7]

Therefore, repentance is a critical ingredient not only to how we begin the Christian life, but how we live out the Christian life, and how we finish the Christian life.

Compelling Change

When genuinely confronting the sin in one's life, a repentant believer realizes something must give, things must change. Repentance is a change of mind that leads to a change in life. To summarize Kevin

4. Keller, *Galatians for You*, 68.
5. Keller, *Galatians for You*, 68–69.
6. Keller, *Galatians for You*, 69.
7. DeYoung, *What Does the Bible Really Teach?*, 98–99.

DeYoung's multifaceted definition of repentance, "you change your mind about yourself, you change your mind about your sin, you change your mind about God, and then you change."[8] Transformation is an indispensable mark of true repentance.

The essence of repentance is consenting to be changed. Surrendering to Christ as Lord is an act of giving over the wheel, of relinquishing the driver's position in your life. You may recall the once-popular bumper sticker that read "God is my copilot." At first, this sounds like a good philosophy. It conveys a message that the Creator of the universe is driving along with you, in cooperation with you, yet subservient in the final analysis of decision-making. However, when you understand biblical repentance, the idea is utterly ridiculous. That a person actually believes, and is willing to promote, the Lord and Sovereign of the universe is in control of, say, 50 percent of my life as a Christian is ludicrous. The apostle Paul, in Col 3, provides a poignant and practical charge regarding the practice of compelling change. Consequently, as J. I. Packer asserts, "A [surrender and] willingness to be changed by Christ remains the fundamental element in all genuine Christian practice."[9] Colossians 3:1–14 says,

> If then you have been raised with Christ, seek the things that are above, where Christ is, seated at the right hand of God. Set your minds on things that are above, not on things that are on earth. For you have died, and your life is hidden with Christ in God. When Christ who is your life appears, then you also will appear with him in glory. Put to death therefore what is earthly in you: sexual immorality, impurity, passion, evil desire, and covetousness, which is idolatry. On account of these the wrath of God is coming. In these you too once walked, when you were living in them. But now you must put them all away: anger, wrath, malice, slander, and obscene talk from your mouth. Do not lie to one another, seeing that you have put off the old self with its practices and have put on the new self, which is being renewed in knowledge after the

8. DeYoung, *What Does the Bible Really Teach?*, 99–100.

9. Packer, *Growing in Christ*, 145.

image of its creator. Here there is not Greek and Jew, circumcised and uncircumcised, barbarian, Scythian, slave, free; but Christ is all, and in all. Put on then, as God's chosen ones, holy and beloved, compassionate hearts, kindness, humility, meekness, and patience, bearing with one another and, if one has a complaint against another, forgiving each other; as the Lord has forgiven you, so you also must forgive. And above all these put on love, which binds everything together in perfect harmony.

In several of his letters, Paul begins with the indicative, who and what we are in Christ, the orthodoxy of our beliefs. He then completes the latter half with the imperative, how and why we should behave and live, the orthopraxy of our faith in Christ. The letter to the church at Colossae is no exception. As chapter 3 begins, Paul turns to the imperative by beginning with the transition "If then," or as some translations read, "Since, then." He begins with the foundational reality of our position as redeemed, spiritually resurrected followers of Christ. To demonstrate the reality of who believers are and to further his argument, the apostle Paul uses phrases such as "raised with Christ" (v. 1) and "hidden in Christ" (v. 3). In other words, if we have been spiritually resurrected (born again), there will be visible consequences of that resurrection.

In verse 2 Paul implores us, "set your minds on things above." It sounds simple, "set your mind" on something, but it is a powerful tool with which God has gifted us. As John Piper notes, "One of the most remarkable capacities of the human mind is the capacity to direct its attention to something it chooses. It is an amazing power, a gift from God."[10] Our actions are most often determined, if not always determined, by that to which we have set our minds. This powerful capacity of our mind's ability to focus and to consider, which then leads to action, is a critical component to godly change. Once more, Piper says, "This is the path toward change. We are called to take it and not wait passively while our minds are

---

10. Piper, *Godward Life*, 228–29.

drawn away with all kinds of passions that wage war against our souls (I Peter 2:11)."[11]

In the verses that follow, the apostle provides two categories in the process of change: "putting off" (vv. 5–10) and "putting on" (vv. 12–14). Beginning in verse 5, Scripture declares examples of what to "put to death" or put off: a litany of sins and sinful behaviors that the follower of Christ must strive to get rid of in their lives. Sins such as sexual immorality, impurity, anger, slander, obscene talk. This list is not meant to be exhaustive, rather representative. Paul then contrasts this reality with what the Christian should put on. These are godly characteristics and behaviors such as "compassionate hearts, kindness, humility, meekness, and patience, bearing with one another and, if one has a complaint against another, forgiving each other." This list is not an exhaustive one of Christian character and behavior, but examples of what mark the life of a disciple of Jesus Christ. This model is what God's word provides as the process of change.

The following exercise is an example of putting off and putting on as a Christian. Let us say you have a problem with anger. It is Sunday morning, and you have gathered with others for worship at the church of which you are a part. Your pastor is preaching through Colossians, and he comes to the passage mentioned above, Col 3:1–14. While listening, verses 7 and 8 really stick out to you: "In these you too once walked, when you were living in them. But now you must put them all away: anger, wrath, malice, slander, and obscene talk from your mouth." You are struck by these words and in your mind, you ponder, "I know I struggle with anger, am short-tempered and say and do things in my anger that I instantly regret. God's word is telling me I once walked as an angry person, and I am not that way anymore, by God's grace. Furthermore, it tells me to put away my anger; make it a point to stop being so angry." But then you are wondering, "How do I just stop being angry?" However, the better question is "Why do I get angry so often?"

---

11. Piper, Godward Life, 229.

What do you do next? As you continue listening to the sermon, verses 12 and 13 of Col 3 resonate in your ears: "Put on then, as God's chosen ones, holy and beloved, compassionate hearts, kindness, humility, meekness, and patience, bearing with one another and, if one has a complaint against another, forgiving each other; as the Lord has forgiven you, so you also must forgive" (vv. 12–13). It is, you admit, your unwillingness to bear with others and forgive others. In other words, it is a selfish heart that you must ask the Lord to renew. More than this, you realize you must ask the Lord to replace what you have taken off. You remember it is the clean and empty places the devil and his demons love to play (Matt 12:43–45). In the place of anger and selfishness, you ask the Lord to grant you a compassionate and forgiving heart.

Here, in Col 3, Scripture reveals to us the process of change: putting off our sins (e.g.—anger) and putting on Christ's character (e.g.—a compassionate and forgiving heart). So, when you get up on Monday morning, you ask the Lord to give you the strength, by his Spirit, to take your selfish disposition and angry responses and replace them with a compassionate and forgiving heart, one that is akin to him and unlike how you have been living. Then, actively look for him to do this in you, moment by moment, day by day. This exercise in transformation is but one example from God's word regarding the critical practice of compelling change in the life of a repentant believer.

Thomas Chalmers, nineteenth-century Scottish minister, reiterates this reality in his sermon, *The Expulsive Power of a New Affection*. His central argument is that a person's heart, the core of their being, is inhabited by desires and affections that can only be displaced by being prevailed upon by a more worthy and attractive affection or desire. Chalmers asserts,

> If to be without desire and without exertion altogether, is a state of violence and discomfort, then the present desire, with its correspondent train of exertion, is not to be got rid of simply by destroying it. It must be by substituting another desire, and another line or habit of exertion in its place—and the most effectual way of withdrawing

the mind from one object, is not by turning it away upon desolate and unpeopled vacancy—but by presenting to its regards another object still more alluring.[12]

Chalmers argues that we replace our sinful and selfish desires by not what is more alluring, but most alluring, namely the Lord Jesus Christ. With Christ as one's greatest treasure change is not only possible, but inevitable. Read the good words of Chalmers again:

> Tell a man to be holy and how can he compass such a performance, when his alone fellowship with holiness is a fellowship of despair? It is the atonement of the cross reconciling the holiness of the lawgiver with the safety of the offender, that hath opened the way for a sanctifying influence into the sinner's heart; and he can take a kindred impression from the character of God now brought nigh, and now at peace with him. Separate the demand from the doctrine; and you have either a system of righteousness that is impracticable, or a barren orthodoxy. Bring the demand and the doctrine together—and the true disciple of Christ is able to do the one, through the other strengthening him. The motive is adequate to the movement; and the bidden obedience of the Gospel is not beyond the measure of his strength, just because the doctrine of the Gospel is not beyond the measure of his acceptance.[13]

To explain Chalmers's biblical assertions, think of the apostle Paul's words in Phil 2:12–13: "Therefore, my beloved, as you have always obeyed, so now, not only as in my presence but much more in my absence, work out your own salvation with fear and trembling, for it is God who works in you, both to will and to work for his good pleasure." It is the Christian who works out his salvation because God has worked in him to do his will and good pleasure. This, my friends, is the practice of compelling change.

12. Chalmers, "Discourse IX," 2.
13. Chalmers, "Discourse IX," 7–8.

Continuous Practice

After reading what is above, you may be thinking, "Is this simply a formula or ritual that I perform, and voila, my sin disappears, and godliness takes its place? Furthermore, what if my vengeful anger (or other sin) returns, what then?" These are honest and important questions. The short answer is, of course not. It is not a magical method, but a spiritual discipline. More than that, it is a lifestyle of intentional decision-making and reprioritizing to align our lives with Christ's will and way. Change and growth take time. Change is gradual, mysterious, and inevitable in the life of a Christian. These questions and responses lead to another critical habit of the repentant believer; namely, continuous practice.

This term is derived from Heb 5:14 which asserts, "But solid food is for the mature, for those who have their powers of discernment trained by *constant practice* to distinguish good from evil." This one verse provides tremendous insight into the life of a disciple who has committed to the challenges and effort it takes to see godly change and growth produced in them. The author of Hebrews describes the maturation process using the analogy of the progression of food a person consumes as they grow, from milk (v. 13) to solid food (v. 14). In that process, there are habits that are formed, practice and training that take place. Recognize the phrase *constant practice*. This phrase is significant to the meaning of the text as well as to understanding the process of growth as a disciple of Jesus. The term connotes the idea of a consistency and regularity in the spiritual diet and digestion of working and walking in the ways of Christ. This phrase and verse clearly imply that discerning good and evil can often be a difficult and complex task. If not, the Christian would not need continuous practice to sharpen their powers of discernment.

A Christian's powers of discernment, having a clear understanding of right and wrong, good and evil, are developed and honed by continuous practice. As New Testament scholar Donald Guthrie explains, "Spiritual maturity comes neither from isolated events nor from a great spiritual burst. It comes from a steady application of spiritual discipline."[14] In particular, it is the spiritual discipline of reading, meditating, understanding, and applying the word of God. In Heb 5:13 the author describes an immature Christian as one who is on milk and is unskilled in the word of righteousness. In contrast, the mature believer is one who consumes the solid food of God's word and is thereby a skilled user of it. Growth and maturity in the life of a believer occurs, in great part, by saturating your thinking in Scripture on a continual basis. Kevin Vanhoozer, in his book *Hearers & Doers*, provides a beautiful description of this process:

> A disciple is a person who is learning Christ. It's a more ambitious subject than astronomy, history, physics, and philosophy combined, for Christ is the culmination of God's plan and the summation of God's wisdom as the gathering place of all things in heaven and earth (Eph 1:10). To learn Christ is to learn to read the Scriptures as testimony to his person and work. To read rightly involves learning doctrine, the treasury of the apostolic tradition, as well (2 Thess 2:15). To read rightly, we must also learn what it means to follow him in our contemporary context.[15]

To mature in Christ, it takes discipline, experience, and time. A follower of Jesus must determine to consistently and continually train their faculties to discern good and evil, growing in the grace and knowledge of Christ, to live a life pleasing to God. Author Joe Rigney reflects on C. S. Lewis's perspective regarding this reality: "Every moment of every day, you are confronted with a choice— either place God at the center of your life, or place something else there."[16] It is a purposing in your heart to immerse yourself in the truths of Scripture long enough that they become part of who you are and how you live. As a result, the decisions you make and the priorities you set are in alignment with God's word and will. This

14. Guthrie, *Hebrews*, 139.

15. Vanhoozer, *Hearers & Doers*, 69.

16. Rigney, *Lewis on the Christian Life*, 29.

consistent conviction and associated behavior are what make up *continuous practice* in the life of a Christ follower.

Consistent Community

American singer, songwriter, and storyteller Tom T. Hall wrote a song entitled "Me and Jesus."[17] This song, and in particular the chorus, epitomizes many Christians' attitudes and dispositions in the West. I call it Tom T. Hall theology. The song captures a philosophy and conviction that all I need to know about being a Christian, I can figure out on my own, just me and Jesus. A purely individualistic view of Christianity is quite pervasive among those who, as a result of adhering to such a philosophy, have an indifferent connection to the local church and appear uncommitted to attendance, participation, and serving, and ultimately disregard most of the New Testament as being written to churches, for churches, and encourages consistent community among God's people (Rom 1:7; 1 Cor 1:2; 2 Cor 1:1; Gal 1:2; Eph 1:1; Phil 1:1; Col 1:2; 1 Thess 1:1; 2 Thess 1:1; 1 Pet 1:1; 2 Pet 1:1; 2 John 1:1; Jude 1:1; Rev 1:4).

A critical practice of a believer is a commitment to consistent community. Following Christ is not an isolated event or journey. Jesus consists in forming a fellowship. The community that Jesus forms is not a nameless and faceless mass, but a community of individuals whose names are known, burdens are shared, and life is lived together. The community is the local church. It is the gathered believers worshipping and doing life together. As Kevin Vanhoozer explains, "The church is the primary location for transforming minds, hearts, and practices."[18] This practice furthers authentic repentance. It is where change best takes place, with and supported by other Christians. In his book *Mere Christianity*, C. S. Lewis asserts, "The Church exists for nothing else but to draw [people] into Christ, to make them little Christs."[19] Regular, com-

---

17. The song can be heard here: https://www.youtube.com/watch?v=5bsfn4_wB4M.

18. Vanhoozer, *Hearers & Doers*, 94.

19. Lewis, *Mere Christianity*, 199.

mitted participation in authentic community fosters true transformation in the life of a repentant follower of Christ. The church is God's chosen medium for his people. It is the place where we worship God and where love for each other originates and develops.

Community occurs as an outgrowth from a commitment to gather with other believers to worship the one true God. More specifically, Mark Dever argues, "Authentic, gospel-revealing community with supernatural depth and breadth is a natural outgrowth of belief in God's Word."[20] As a follower of Jesus is met by the power of God's word, not only by his own study of it, but by a regular diet of Scripture from the teaching and preaching of the leaders of the local church, that follower begins to change and form significant and lasting relationships with other disciples who are doing the same. As Dever continues to explain, "Discipleship involves a significant, self-conscious commitment to the local church. Scripture has no other concept of Christians."[21] This, my friends, is the plan of God for his followers.

Consider Eph 4:11–12: "And he gave the apostles, the prophets, the evangelists, the shepherds and teachers, to equip the saints for the work of ministry, for building up the body of Christ." Notice, Scripture is telling us that Christ created these offices and called men to these positions, whose primary function is to first preach and teach the word of God, to equip God's people to do the work of ministry. The medium whereby this best and most often occurs is the local church, the community of believers. As Dever and Dunlop promote, "Christ gave the church ministers of the Word not to effect change, but to equip others to effect change."[22] It is in this context that followers of Christ learn how to live, how to interact with one another, and how to apply the word of God during the week ahead, and how the body of believers are built up and transformed.

---

20. Dever and Dunlop, *Compelling Community*, 33.

21. Dever and Dunlop, *Compelling Community*, 62.

22. Dever and Dunlop, *Compelling Community*, 90.

These claims are not mere speculations, but valid and conclusive from the evidence given in the verses that follow in Eph 4. Note verses 13–16:

> Until we all attain to the unity of the faith and of the knowledge of the Son of God, to mature manhood, to the measure of the stature of the fullness of Christ, so that we may no longer be children, tossed to and fro by the waves and carried about by every wind of doctrine, by human cunning, by craftiness in deceitful schemes. Rather, speaking the truth in love, we are to grow up in every way into him who is the head, into Christ, from whom the whole body, joined and held together by every joint with which it is equipped, when each part is working properly, makes the body grow so that it builds itself up in love.

The above verses reveal the results of those who have authentically repented and practice consistent community within the body of Christ followers. Specifically, consistent community existing under the sound teaching and preaching of the Bible fosters unity, a deepening knowledge of Jesus Christ, stability, and a sharpening of spiritual discernment. Further, notice the apostle Paul's use of the body as a metaphor for the local church. When all who follow Christ are connected and committed to one another, spiritual maturity occurs, transformation happens, and growth in love and service takes place. Kevin Vanhoozer highlights this reality by asserting, "[This context produces a] people who are ready, willing, and able to display the mind and wisdom of Christ in every situation by doing the kind of thing Christ commanded, the kind of thing that corresponds to the new reality 'in Christ.'"[23] This model of Christian community, promoted by God's word, is the brand of discipleship that shapes, that sticks, that stays. Living out, adhering to, and following an Eph 4 platform for consistent community is how repentant Christ followers grow into Christlikeness, lovingly speak the truth, and joyfully serve one another so that each one is built up as a body "in every way into him who is the head,

---

23. Vanhoozer, *Hearers & Doers*, 134.

into Christ" (v. 15). The practice of consistent community is vital for those who have repented and are committed to living a life of repentance.

Compassionate Evangelism

As you live a life of repentance, following the practices discussed above, it becomes apparent that there are those in your circle of influence who are in desperate need of the same repentance you have experienced and presently enjoy. You realize and are confronted with the reality from the word of God that the people with whom you work, or go to school, or who are a part of your family, do not know Jesus and are called to repent, even if they are unaware. Yet, how will they know unless those who have repented tell them? This brings me to the fifth and final practice in this chapter discussing the repentant disciple of Jesus: *compassionate evangelism*.

Admittedly, this is not a book on strategies and methods of evangelism. However, this chapter is about the habits and practices of those who have repented of their sins and committed their lives to Jesus. One such practice is that of compassionate evangelism. Seeing others as Christ did, like sheep without a shepherd, and, in turn, pointing those to the Good Shepherd is a worthy command and endeavor. It is an endeavor that, in prayerful hope and evangelistic obedience, will lead them to the Savior and keeper of their souls.

Recall the discussion of Mark 1:15–20 in the first chapter of this book. Jesus preaches repentance and calls his first disciples to come follow him, to repent, begin their journey following the Son of God, and becoming fishers of men. Theologian David Garland, commenting on this reality, asserts,

> Jesus does not call them to be shepherds, gathering in the lost sheep of the house of Israel, or to be laborers, bringing in the sheaves (Matt. 9:36–38), but to be fishers. Old Testament prophets used this metaphor for gathering people for judgment (Jer. 16:14–16; Ezek. 29:4; 47:10; Amos 4:2; Hab. 1:14–17), and one should not

assume that Jesus uses fishing as a benign reference to mission. When the fisherman hooks a fish, it has fatal consequences for the fish; life cannot go on as before. This image fits the transforming power of God's rule that brings judgment and death to the old, yet promises a new creation (see Rom. 6:1–11). The disciples are called to be agents who will bring a compelling message to others that will change their lives beyond recognition.[24]

What a powerful and sobering reality. That we, as Jesus's disciples are called to an enterprise that is not passive, but very much active; not apathy, but passion in how we live and what we say, all for the one who has hooked us, as it were. Furthermore, New Testament scholar William Lane explains,

> The immediate function of those called to be fishers of men is to accompany Jesus as witnesses to the proclamation of the nearness of the kingdom and the necessity for men to turn to God through radical repentance. Their ultimate function [and ours] will be to confront men with God's decisive action, which to faith has the character of salvation, but to unbelief has the character of judgment.[25]

Jesus's call and claim on the lives of his followers is so compelling that it not only transforms his adherents, but further, it changes the way you and I view others.

Recall the apostle Paul's words in 2 Cor 5:14–16:

> For the love of Christ controls us, because we have concluded this: that one has died for all, therefore all have died; and he died for all, that those who live might no longer live for themselves but for him who for their sake died and was raised. From now on, therefore, we regard no one according to the flesh. Even though we once regarded Christ according to the flesh, we regard him thus no longer.

24. Garland, *Mark*, 62.
25. Lane, *Mark*, 11.

Notice Paul's logic and line of thought. As followers of Christ, we are controlled by the love of Christ. He is the one who gave himself, vicariously, so that we who are destined for eternal death may now be destined for eternal life. Therefore, we no longer live for ourselves, but for the one who died for us.

The subsequent conclusion is that we regard no one the same way any longer. The spiritual dynamic of the human psyche is more top of mind to Christians. Eternality of the soul matters more to those who follow Christ, and the fate of those who are unbelievers is a more acute matter of gravitas. Commentator David Garland further explains:

> Understanding the full meaning of the cross and resurrection and fully experiencing the Spirit brings an enlightenment that causes Christians to see things and other persons in new ways. Consequently, Paul now sees others according to their standing with Christ (see Rom 14:8–12) and concedes that all his previous judgments of others were wrong. God's verdict on our sin condemns us all and destroys any illusions of superiority or inferiority. Jew and Greek, slave and free, male and female are all on the same level before God. All share a kinship with one another because of sin but also share kinship with one another because Christ died for all to redeem all. When we see that we are all sinners dead in our sins and needing reconciliation from God.[26]

As with the apostle Paul, we too are called to see people differently, not as mere humans, but eternal beings who need Jesus. This brings with it a deep, heartfelt compassion for those who need Jesus. More than that, if we see others Christ's way, we have a joyful obligation and compulsion to lovingly engage those in our circle of influence with the gospel.

The Great Commission (Matt 28:16–20) is therefore understood as a call to compassion. It is love in action, or as Pastor Paul Hines defines it, "Compassion is sorry with shoes on."[27] The

---

26. Garland, 2 Corinthians, 202.

27. Munfordville BC, "MBC Worship Gathering," 44:36–44:39.

greatest act of love we can display to another person is revealing to them the truth of the gospel. May our resolve as repentant followers of Christ be as the great nineteenth-century Baptist preacher Charles Spurgeon who declared, "If sinners be damned, at least let them leap to hell over our dead bodies. And if they perish, let them perish with our arms wrapped about their knees, imploring them to stay. If hell must be filled, let it be filled in the teeth of our exertions, and let not one go unwarned and unprayed for."[28] May we each be determined to tell others who we know have not yet yielded their lives to Jesus Christ of both the judgement of God that's coming, and the diversion of absorption of God's wrath and forgiveness found in the Savior, Christ Jesus our Lord. It is with those last two words of Spurgeon's declaration, "unprayed for," that leads us to the last chapter of this book.

28. Spurgeon, *Spurgeon's Sermons*, 18.

5

A Posture and Prayer for Repentance

As you come to the last chapter of this book, I want to offer you both a posture towards and a prayer for those who need repentance. My hope and prayer are that by this point you both feel and grasp the weight of the necessity of repentance for all who wish to follow Jesus and make heaven their eternal home. The following pages are written so that you will have a biblically driven, gospel-centered approach of persuading and praying for others who need to repent.

What is believed to be the apostle Paul's last correspondence before martyrdom is that of 2 Timothy. There is a passage within that letter instructing young Pastor Timothy on how to conduct himself among those who oppose the gospel as well as a prayerful hope of what may result. Consider 2 Tim 2:24–26,

> And the Lord's servant must not be quarrelsome but kind to everyone, able to teach, patiently enduring evil, correcting his opponents with gentleness. God may perhaps grant them repentance leading to a knowledge of the truth, and they may come to their senses and escape from the snare of the devil, after being captured by him to do his will.

This passage is a beautiful description of how we, as God's servants, are to act and pray for those who oppose the gospel, who need to repent.

The first sentence of this passage presents the actions and reactions of Christians toward those who do not yet know Christ. As we engage unbelievers, we should not be quarrelsome. Our response to those who oppose Christ is to be one of kindness, not a posture of petulance. Recall the words of Solomon in Prov 15:1, "A soft answer turns away wrath, but a harsh word stirs up anger." John Newton, writing to a friend regarding the disposition of a follower of Jesus, stresses, "He believes and feels his own weakness and unworthiness, and lives upon the grace and pardoning love of his Lord. This gives him an habitual tenderness and gentleness of spirit."[1] Notice Newton is not simply emphasizing tenderness and gentleness, but a habitual tenderness and gentleness. Our kindness and patience must extend beyond a complimentary encounter with those who need Christ; it needs to be a practice. As a habit, our approach towards unbelievers must be with a keen and patient ear, loving instruction, and gentle correction. In so doing, we point others, who may oppose the gospel, towards getting to see the real, unimagined perspective of Christianity so that they would come to know and love Christ. As this process continues, or is repeated, we are hopeful that God the Holy Spirit intervenes in the lives of our unbelieving friends and family, granting them life and the gift of repentance.

Verses 25 and 26 of 2 Timothy detail the spiritual reality of everyone who needs Christ. Carefully notice each aspect of a person's lostness. First, they need the truth, and second, they need to come to their senses. Paul instructs Christians in 2 Cor 4:4 that "In their case the god of this world has blinded the minds of the unbelievers, to keep them from seeing the light of the gospel of the glory of Christ, who is the image of God." The unrepentant are blinded to the truth and are not clear thinkers, spiritually speaking. They have been blinded to the reality of the Savior and why he came. The god of this world, namely Satan and his minions,

1. Newton, *Works of Rev. John Newton*, 170.

are those who hold up the blinders, blocking out the light of the glorious gospel. Further, the apostle tells us in 2 Timothy that unbelievers are snared by the devil, being captured to do his will. Paul uses the word *snare*, a device often used to trap birds, typically by seducing them into the sphere of the snare. Once there, the bird is trapped, unable to get free from the net of the snarer.

The devil uses attractive ideologies, people, events, and the like to ensnare those who oppose the gospel and refuse to repent. Satan does so in order that those he traps do his bidding, his will. It is important to see that these are the realities of those who have not repented from their sins and reject following Christ. Most people tend to land on the extreme ends of what I call the "devil belief scale." Either people believe that the devil does not exist or that he is around every corner and behind every bush. Since extremism usually is offensive to people, many are simply dismissive of the reality of Satan and his demons. Sadly, that position is exactly the one the devil prefers. C. S. Lewis, in his book *Screwtape Letters* explains, "There are two equal and opposite errors into which our race can fall about the devils. One is to disbelieve in their existence. The other is to believe, and to feel an excessive and unhealthy interest in them. They themselves (the devils) are equally pleased by both errors and hail a materialist or a magician with the same delight."[2] A crucial part of our posture towards and prayers for unbelievers involves spiritual warfare, asking God, the Holy Spirit to release them from the trap and dominion of Satan.

In the following paragraphs, I want to offer you two perspectives. One is an illustration of 2 Tim 2:25–26. The second perspective is a suggested method of praying for those you know who need to repent and discover true salvation that is found only in Christ Jesus.

---

2. Lewis, *Screwtape Letters*, 2.

Illustration of 2 Tim 2:24-26

In Luke 15, we find quite possibly the greatest parable of Jesus, what is most popularly called "The Prodigal Son." In my estimation, this story is a beautiful depiction of what has been discussed in the section above. The parable begins in verse 11: "And he said, 'There was a man who had two sons. And the younger of them said to his father, "Father, give me the share of property that is coming to me." And he divided his property between them.'" The younger son went his own way with his inheritance, wishing his father were dead. After a time of going his own way and doing his own thing, inevitably, the son squandered away all his inheritance. He found himself feeding pigs, and so hungry that he longed to eat the slop they were consuming. As John MacArthur puts it, "His freewheeling lifestyle had suddenly morphed into a terrible, crushing bondage. All his dreams had become nightmares. All his fun had given way to profound sorrow. His so-called friends were all gone. It was as bad as it could get, and he was about to die."[3]

Hitting rock bottom is a gracious gift from God. On the way down, almost all of us attempt to fix ourselves. The Prodigal had run out of his inheritance money as well as friends, and therefore thought he would get a job, become a citizen of a new country, and everything might turn around. MacArthur asserts, "That is typical of sinners on the run from God. They often reassure themselves with the notion that they have the means and the ability to work their way out of the mess they have made of their lives. Some people waste years under the delusion, and for many it becomes a pathway of destruction they never escape from."[4] It is quite sad that so many must come to a low point, usually an extremely low one, in life before turning to the source of our eternal salvation. For the Prodigal, it was no different.

In case you did not know, the Prodigal's means and abilities were fruitless. He ends up feeding pigs and is so hungry that he longs for the slop of the pigs (vv. 15–16). It is at this point in the

3. MacArthur, *Tale of Two Sons*, 69.
4. MacArthur, *Tale of Two Sons*, 71.

parable that Jesus explains an epiphany of sorts, a pivotal moment in the life of the Prodigal. Verse 17 begins, "But when he came to himself." It is in this moment that God grants repentance to the Prodigal. On his own, the son would not have turned back to the Father, but in God's mercy, he opened the Prodigal's eyes. He came to his senses and realized the truth (vv. 17–19). He was now ready to submit to his father, to his authority, and his commands. He was willing to do whatever it took to come back home. He was compelled to repent.

The rest of the parable reveals a marvelous account of the Prodigal's return. The father's mercy, grace, and joy in forgiving and receiving his son back home was revealed in his running to his son to greet him, embrace and kiss him, welcoming him home (v. 20). Furthermore, the father had a new set of clothes placed on him, and a feast prepared to celebrate the son's return (vv. 22–23, 32). The son had escaped the snare of the devil and was released to do the father's will. This is repentance. That is what the apostle Paul describes in 2 Timothy.

A Prayer for Repentance

If you are reading this book, it is quite likely that you know someone close to you who does not know Jesus and needs to repent. Perhaps you have said as much to those individuals by having gospel conversations, heart-to-heart talks, and may have even said more than you should. At this point you may wonder, "What else can I say or do?" Well, I am glad you asked.

I want to challenge you to take verses 25 and 26 of 2 Timothy and use them as a prayer to bring before Christ those who need to repent and place their trust in him. Let me remind you of these verses: "God may perhaps grant them repentance leading to a knowledge of the truth, and they may come to their senses and escape from the snare of the devil, after being captured by him to do his will." God's word gives us a four-pronged progression of what it takes for someone to come to the point of repentance. Consequently, that is why these verses are so poignant and powerful to pray over those who are not yet followers of Jesus. The following paragraphs break down these four areas into focal points of prayer.

The first part of our prayer is that *God may grant them repentance*. We must always remember that it is a supernatural act when a person turns from their sin to salvation in Christ alone. As such, it is God who must grant the gift of repentance. None of us can manipulate circumstances or muster enough good will to cause another to repent, only God can do that. Because repentance is a gift from God, it is all the more reason you and I must pray for those who need Christ, who need to turn from their sins and way of living and turn to the living Son of God. Realizing this biblical perspective, let us plead with our Lord to move in their lives, open their eyes to their sin, and cause them to turn from it to him.

Recall Cornelius and Lydia in the book of Acts that was discussed in chapter 3 of this book. In the case of Cornelius, it was God who orchestrated the events and circumstances that led to not only himself, but his entire household repenting. It is worth repeating Acts 11:18 here: "When they heard these things they fell silent. And they glorified God, saying, 'Then to the Gentiles also God has granted repentance that leads to life.'" In a similar manner, Lydia came to repentance and saving faith on the banks of the river outside the city of Philippi. Remember, during Paul's second missionary journey, the apostle was headed to the churches he had established in Asia Minor, but after going through Phrygia and Galatia, the Holy Spirit prevented them from going any further in their planned direction. Instead, Paul was given a vision in the night by the Spirit. In the vision, a man was calling for help from Macedonia, a region he had not planned to visit. Paul and his companions eventually arrived in the principal city of Philippi and there met Lydia and others on the banks of the river during the Sabbath. Acts 16:14 records, "One who heard us was a woman named Lydia, from the city of Thyatira, a seller of purple goods, who was a worshiper of God. The Lord opened her heart to pay attention to what was said by Paul." It was the Lord who opened her heart to hear and be saved. Beloved, for this is what we must earnestly pray. Pray that God would grant repentance and open hearts to hear, to see, to repent, and to believe.

Second, is to pray for the unrepentant *to be led to the truth*. In the latter part of Rom 1, the apostle Paul begins to explain the disposition of the unrighteous. Among his explanation are these words, "they exchanged the truth about God for a lie" (v. 25). The unrighteous have chosen to believe a lie, namely that although they knew God, they did not honor God and their foolish hearts were darkened. Even in these words, it is often difficult for you and me to believe that those who have not repented are believing and living a lie. It is with this in mind that our prayer should be requesting that God would lead them to a knowledge of the truth. Pray for those you know and love that are without Jesus to see their true spiritual state: dark, desolate, desperate, dead. Pray that they would realize the error of their ways, and realizing their path is a pathway of lies would turn toward the reality of Christ to the pathway of truth. Even while you are praying these words, you may come to a deeper understanding and appreciation, as I have, that it is truly, and only, God who can awaken the spiritual senses to see and come to grips with the horrifying reality that "I have been wrong and going the wrong way all this time." Pray that our Lord, in his tender mercies, would clearly lead those who need him to that truth. This prayer is an eager expectation for the next step in the process of praying for the lost, namely *coming to their senses*.

Thirdly then, our prayers for those in need of repentance is that they *come to their senses*. Those who are without Christ, who have often engendered false and even evil ideologies are in a spiritually inebriated state. Often, their way of thinking and being acts as a potent soporific or narcotic. As New Testament scholar Philip Towner points out, "[Repentance] is described as a sobering-up, which in moral discussions depicts a coming to one's senses."[5] While this concept may sound alarmist or even extreme to those who do not see the seriousness of sin and it's resulting in separation from God, it is a reality for which we must come to grips. First Corinthians 2:14 reminds, "The natural person does not accept the

5. Towner, *Letters to Timothy and Titus*, 276.

things of the Spirit of God, for they are folly to him, and he is not able to understand them because they are spiritually discerned." Anything that is of spiritual and eternal value, an unbeliever sees no worth or wisdom in accepting or understanding those things. As Scripture reminds us, they are foolishness to someone without Christ. That is why it is so critical to pray that the unrepentant person comes to their spiritual senses.

Fourthly, our prayers for the unrepentant must include a pleading with God *to release them from both the snare of the devil and the desire to do the will of the evil one.* The apostle Paul reminds us in verse 26 of 2 Tim 2 that those who oppose the gospel have an insurmountable need: "[to] escape from the snare of the devil, after being captured by him to do his will." The Bible's words reveal the seriousness of an unrepentant heart, including the depths of deception Satan and this world deploys on those without Christ. It is a terrible, yet sobering reality that the devil is at work taking captive and using for his purposes those who oppose the gospel. Humanly speaking, none of us can escape the trap of the devil, only God can set a person free from Satan's snare. To that end, we should pray fervently for the ultimate freedom found only in turning to and embracing the Savior.

With all this in mind, may I suggest the following prayer:

> Lord Jesus, I honor and hallow your name. I thank you that you have enabled me to approach you, and you listen, and you deeply care. Today, I am lifting [Person's Name] to your throne of grace. I pray for [Person's Name] that you may grant them repentance. Lord Jesus, I pray that you lead them to a knowledge of the truth, causing them to come to their senses. Lord, I plead with you to provide [Person's Name] an escape from the snare of the devil. It is my prayerful longing that you would release them from Satan's will that they may do Yours. This is my prayer. Amen.

To be clear, this is not a formula for someone's coming to repentance. Consider this prayer as a template, a model of sorts. This prayer will biblically guide you to pray 2 Tim 2:25–26 for those who need Christ. Specifically, my challenge to you is to pray this prayer for at least one person, every day for the next thirty days. There are two reasons why. One, is so that you are intentionally and consistently praying for someone among those you know and love that need Jesus. This pleases God (Rom 10:1; 11:13–14). The second reason is that thirty days of praying for someone to turn to Christ is bound to have a compassionate effect on you. Your attitude and willingness to reach out to that person with a church invite, a gospel conversation, and the like will grow in tandem with the number of days and times you are praying for that person.

Remember the purpose of your character, actions, and prayers as God's servant; namely, that God may grant repentance to those who have not yet believed. Furthermore, we must always keep in mind the power and reach of the Savior. I want to end this chapter with two compelling quotes to grab your attention and your heart when it comes to praying for the lost. In his article "Confidence and Contentment in Prayer," John Onwuchekwa poignantly asserts,

> Hear me. We won't consistently pray if we're not sure of God's ability. So much of our failure to pray comes from subtly believing that within God exists the possibility of failure. Because of this, we never ask God to do the impossible. Instead, we pursue only the things we can accomplish on our own.[6]

Lord, may we trust you more fully, knowing you can do the impossible and cannot fail.

The second quote comes from George Mueller. In his autobiography, he writes the following concerning prayer for the unconverted:

> I am now, in 1864, waiting upon God for certain blessings, for which I have daily besought Him for 19 years and 6 months, without one day's intermission. Still the full answer is not yet given concerning the conversion of certain individuals. In the meantime, I have received many thousands of answers to prayer. I have also prayed

6. Onwuchekwa, "Confidence and Contentment in Prayer," para. 6.

daily, without intermission, for the conversion of other individuals about ten years, for others six or seven years, for others four, three, and two years, for others about eighteen months; and still the answer is not yet granted, concerning these persons [for whom I have prayed for nineteen years and six months]. Yet I am daily continuing in prayer and expecting the answer. Be encouraged, dear Christian reader, with fresh earnestness to give yourself to prayer, if you can only be sure that you ask for things which are for the glory of God.[7]

As we who are Christ followers live our lives, may we do so with a sensitivity to the unrepentant who the Lord has placed in our circle of influence. May we be diligent and intentional to pray for them on a regular basis with a biblical and gospel-centered perspective and fervency, knowing that God can indeed do the impossible.

---

7. Mueller, *Life of Trust*, 296.

Conclusion

As you reach the end of this book, my prayer is that you are encouraged by the light shone on the beautiful gift of repentance. It is my desire that you retain three truths concerning repentance.

1. The Biblical Meaning of Repentance

Recall that repentance is both an event and a journey. It is a moment in which God grants the gift of turning, of transformation. It is the beginning of true and eternal life. At that point, a person not only may repent, but can repent (John 6:37, 44). A turning from one's sin and selfish living, to Christ and righteous living because of what he has done for us. As Packer puts it, "Repentance, in the broadest sense, signifies the change of mind, purpose, attitude, and behavior whereby we embrace God's agenda of mercy toward us and turning back from the old life of fighting God by playing God to live the new life of humbly and thankfully serving Him."[1]

2. A Picture of Repentance

Whether it is Zacchaeus in Luke's Gospel or Lydia in Acts, my prayer is that you have been captivated by the God-initiating, God-granting, grace-giving, life-changing portraits of repentance. Remember, from a human perspective, this is often the unanticipated expectation of the Lord. Think about this reality: that God would come along in time and choose someone like Cornelius, like us, mere sinners, to be

---

1. Packer, *Taking Repentance Seriously*, 7.

a part of his kingdom, and, in a broader sense, the amazing reality that Christ gave himself on a cross to die for our sins, in the place that we deserve, to save us, to make us his own. Further, that we, in turn, would turn to him in response and trust him to be who he says he is: Savior and Lord, protector, provider, the eternal and perfect God. What a marvelous picture of his sovereignty and divine orchestration to remove cultural barriers, soften hearts, intersect lives, save sinners.

3. **A Prayer for Repentance**

It is inevitable that we all have someone that we know and love who has yet to believe, who needs to repent. I pray and encourage you to use 2 Tim 2:25–26 as template for earnestly praying for that person, or persons, who desperately need to turn to Christ. And, as consistently and fervently praying for others often does, we are changed, drawn closer to Jesus, and have a bolder evangelistic zeal as a result. Here again, is an example of the prayer:

> Lord Jesus, I honor and hallow your name. I thank you that you have enabled me to approach you, and that you listen, and you deeply care. Today, I am lifting [Person's Name] to your throne of grace. I pray for [Person's Name] that you may grant them repentance. Lord Jesus, I pray that you lead them to a knowledge of the truth, causing them to come to their senses. Lord, I plead with you to provide [Person's Name] an escape from the snare of the devil. That they would be released from Satan's will that they may do Yours. This is my prayer. Amen.

Bibliography

Bloom, Jon. "The Cost of Nondiscipleship." *Desiring God*, August 5, 2016. https://www.desiringgod.org/articles/the-cost-of-nondiscipleship.

Bock, Darrell L. *Acts*. Baker Exegetical Commentary on the New Testament. Grand Rapids, MI: Baker Academic, 2010.

———. *Luke: The NIV Application Commentary from Biblical Text—to Contemporary Life*. NIV Application Commentary. Grand Rapids, MI: Zondervan, 1996.

Bonhoeffer, Dietrich. *The Cost of Discipleship*. Translated by R. H. Fuller. Rev. ed. New York: Macmillan, 1963.

Calvin, John. *Institutes of the Christian Religion*. Translated by Henry Beveridge. Peabody, MA: Hendrickson, 2008.

"The Canons of Dort." https://www.crcna.org/welcome/beliefs/confessions/canons-dort.

Carmichael, Amy. *Things as They Are*. N.p.: CreateSpace, 2013.

Chalmers, Thomas. "Discourse IX: 'The Expulsive Power of a New Affection.'" https://www.cslewisinstitute.org/wp-content/uploads/ExpulsivePoweDiscourseIX.pdf.

Cole, R. Alan. *Mark: An Introduction and Commentary*. Tyndale New Testament Commentaries 2. Nottingham, UK: InterVarsity, 2008.

Crossway. "What Is Repentance?" *YouTube*, January 11, 2016. https://www.youtube.com/watch?v=gExLXpPJDd8.

Dever, Mark, and Jamie Dunlop. *The Compelling Community: Where God's Power Makes a Church Attractive*. IX Marks. Wheaton, IL: Crossway, 2015.

DeYoung, Kevin. "Godly Grief." *The Gospel Coalition* (blog), June 4, 2010. https://www.thegospelcoalition.org/blogs/kevin-deyoung/godly-grief/.

———. *What Does the Bible Really Teach about Homosexuality?* Wheaton, IL: Crossway, 2015.

———. "Worldly Grief." *The Gospel Coalition* (blog), June 1, 2010. https://www.thegospelcoalition.org/blogs/kevin-deyoung/worldly-grief/.

Garland, David E. *2 Corinthians*. New American Commentary 29. Nashville, TN: Broadman & Holman, 1999.

Guthrie, Donald. *Hebrews: An Introduction and Commentary.* Tyndale New Testament Commentaries 15. Downers Grove: InterVarsity, 2009.

Hughes, R. Kent. *Luke: That You May Know the Truth, ESV Edition.* Wheaton, IL: Crossway, 2014.

———. *2 Corinthians: Power in Weakness.* Wheaton, IL: Crossway, 2006.

Keller, Timothy. *Galatians for You.* Purcellville, VA: The Good Book, 2013.

Keller, Timothy, and Allen Thompson. *Church Planter Manual.* New York: Redeemer Church Planting Center, 2002.

Kruse, Colin G. *2 Corinthians: An Introduction and Commentary.* Tyndale New Testament Commentaries 8. Nottingham, UK: InterVarsity, 2015.

Lane, William L. *The Gospel according to Mark.* The New International Commentary on the New Testament. Grand Rapids, MI: Eerdmans, 2010.

Lawson, Steven J. *The Heroic Boldness of Martin Luther.* A Long Line of Godly Men Profile. Orlando, FL: Reformation Trust, 2013.

Lewis, C. S. *Mere Christianity: Comprising the Case for Christianity, Christian Behaviour, and beyond Personality.* New York: Simon & Schuster, 1996.

———. *The Screwtape Letters.* 1942. Reprint, London: Collins, 2012.

Luther, Martin. "Explanation of the Ninety-Five Theses." http://www.oocities.org/united_in_christ_3in1/95explained.pdf.

———. *Martin Luther's Ninety-Five Theses.* Edited by Stephen J. Nichols. Phillipsburg, NJ: P & R, 2021.

MacArthur, John. *A Tale of Two Sons: The Inside Story of a Father, His Sons, and a Shocking Murder.* Nashville, TN: Nelson, 2008.

Morris, Leon. *Luke.* Tyndale New Testament Commentaries 3. Nottingham, UK: InterVarsity, 2008.

Müller, George. *The Life of Trust.* N.p.: Independently published, 2019.

Munfordville BC. "MBC Worship Gathering." *YouTube,* September 11, 2022. https://www.youtube.com/watch?v=moJqaEgEMHA.

Newton, John. *The Works of the Rev. John Newton.* Vol. 1. London: Wentworth, 2016.

Onwuchekwa, John. "Confidence and Contentment in Prayer." *Radical* (blog), March 27, 2019. https://radical.net/article/confidence-and-contentment-in-prayer/.

Packer, J. I. *Growing in Christ.* Vereeniging, South Africa: Christian Art, 2009.

———. *Taking Repentance Seriously.* Ontario: Anglican Network in Canada, 2007.

Piper, John. *A Godward Life: Book Two, Savoring the Sustenance of God in All of Life.* Sisters, OR: Multnomah, 1999.

Rigney, Joe. *Lewis on the Christian Life: Becoming Truly Human in the Presence of God.* Theologians on the Christian Life. Wheaton, IL: Crossway, 2018.

Schnabel, Eckhard J. *Acts: Zondervan Exegetical Commentary on the New Testament.* Grand Rapids, MI: Zondervan, 2012.

Shelley, Bruce L. *Church History in Plain Language.* Dallas, TX: Word, 2008.

Spurgeon, Charles Haddon. *Spurgeon's Sermons, Volume 7: 1861.* N.p.: Lulu, 2017.

Stein, Robert H. *Mark*. Baker Exegetical Commentary on the New Testament. Grand Rapids, MI: Baker Academic, 2008.

Stevenson, Burton Egbert, ed. *The Macmillan Book of Proverbs, Maxims, and Famous Phrases*. 5th ed. New York: Macmillan, 1965.

Towner, Philip H. *The Letters to Timothy and Titus*. Grand Rapids, MI: Eerdmans, 2009.

Vanhoozer, Kevin J. *Hearers and Doers: A Pastor's Guide to Making Disciples through Scripture and Doctrine*. Bellingham, WA: Lexham, 2019.

Watson, Thomas. *The Doctrine of Repentance*. 1668. Reprint, New York: Banner of Truth, 1994.

Wells, David F. *Turning to God: Biblical Conversion in the Modern World*. Exeter, UK: Paternoster, 1989.

Printed in the USA
CPSIA information can be obtained
at www.ICGtesting.com
LVHW021539310124
770461LV00003B/91